W9-BAH-556

# A SURVIVAL GUIDE FOR STUDENTS:

## TIPS FROM THE TRENCHES

# A SURVIVAL GUIDE FOR STUDENTS:

## TIPS FROM THE TRENCHES

*by Alan Gelb and Karen Levine*

**THOMSON**

—————✶————— ™

**DELMAR LEARNING**

Australia Canada Mexico Singapore Spain United Kingdom United States

## THOMSON

### DELMAR LEARNING

**Survival Guide for Students**
by Alan Gelb and Karen Levine

**Vice President, Career Education SBU:**
Dawn Gerran

**Director of Editorial:**
Sherry Gomoll

**Developmental Editor:**
Pat Gillivan

**Director of Production:**
Wendy A. Troeger

**Production Coordinator:**
Nina Tucciarelli

**Director of Marketing:**
Donna J. Lewis

**Channel Manager:**
Wendy Mapstone

**Composition:**
Type Shoppe II
    Productions, Ltd.

COPYRIGHT © 2004 by Delmar Learning, a
division ofThomson Learning, Inc. Thomson
Learning™ is a trademark used herein under
license

Printed in Canada
1 2 3 4 5 XXX 07 06 05 04 03

For more information contact Delmar,
5 Maxwell Drive
CLIFTON PARK, NY 12065-2919
at http://www.EarlyChildEd.delmar.com

ALL RIGHTS RESERVED. No part of this work covered by the copyright hereon may be reproduced
or used in any form or by any means—graphic,
electronic, or mechanical, including photocopying,
recording, taping, Web distribution or information
storage and retrieval systems—without written
permission of the publisher.

For permission to use material from this text or
product, contact us by
Tel     (800) 730-2214
Fax     (800) 730-2215
www.thomsonrights.com

**Library of Congress
Cataloging-in-Publication Data**
ISBN: 1-4018-3226-1

### NOTICE TO THE READER

Publisher does not warrant or guarantee any of the products described herein or perform any inde-
pendent analysis in connection with any of the product information contained herein. Publisher does
not assume, and expressly disclaims, any obligation to obtain and include information other than that
provided to it by the manufacturer.

The reader is expressly warned to consider and adopt all safety precautions that might be indicated
by the activities herein and to avoid all potential hazards. By following the instructions contained herein, the reader willingly assumes all risks in connection with such instructions.

The Publisher makes no representation or warranties of any kind, including but not limited to, the warranties of fitness for particular purpose or merchantability, nor are any such representations implied
with respect to the material set forth herein, and the publisher takes no responsibility with respect to
such material. The publisher shall not be liable for any special, consequential, or exemplary damages
resulting, in whole or part, from the readers' use of, or reliance upon, this material.

# CONTENTS

Chapter 1: Getting Off on the Right Foot ......1

Chapter 2: Staying on Track ..........................23

Chapter 3: The Goal Zone ............................39

Chapter 4: It's All in Your Mind ....................55

Chapter 5: Study Skills ................................75

Chapter 6: Testing and Other High Stress
Events ..........................................93

Chapter 7: Getting Organized .....................113

Chapter 8: Works and Plays Well
with Others..................................131

Chapter 9: Say It and Hear It .......................149

Chapter 10: Holistic Hints ...........................167

Chapter 11: All About Money .......................195

Chapter 12: The Job in Your Future..............221

Index: ...................................................241

# Acknowledgments

The authors and Delmar would like to express our gratitude to the following professionals who offered numerous valuable suggestions:

*Marianne Fitzpatrick*
Bauder College
Atlanta, Georgia

*Aleyenne Johnson-Jonas*
Maric College
Vista, California

*Dena King*
Nebraska College of Business
Omaha, Nebraska

*Peter Rhein*
Lincoln Technical Institute
Philadelphia, Pennsylvania

*Joseph S. Spadafora, Jr.*
Lincoln Technical Institute
Philadelphia, Pennsylvania

## Chapter 1

# GETTING OFF ON THE RIGHT FOOT

Here you are back in school, and you've probably got a whole lot of feelings to sort out, haven't you? Are you happy? Excited? Bored? Restless? Are you somehow feeling a little bit of everything all at once? If so, don't worry about it. Most students have a complicated love-hate relationship with school, so why should you be any different?

School makes demands on you; there is no getting around that. At other times in your life, you may have resisted those demands. In adolescence, for instance, it is quite typical to resent the demands that school makes on you, as well as those put forth by your parents and other significant adults. For some people, this adolescent resistance can turn into a tornado of feelings that may take years to blow away.

There are many other factors that can generate complicated feelings about school as well. Take learning disabilities, for instance. If not handled properly, learning disabilities can sour a person on school at a very early age. Still other students feel a pull away from school in so many different directions. Perhaps family finances require students to earn an income at the expense of school time. Perhaps a special talent like sports or music takes center stage, leaving academic pursuits in the background.

What we do know is that school is meant to be for everyone, not just the privileged few who sail through it. A school that does its job well manages to find ways to motivate *all* of its students. But students have to meet their schools halfway. They have to discover their own reservoir of motivation and draw on it to achieve. We will be talking more about motivation in the coming chapters, but let's take a moment to think about it here. Are there any issues standing between you and your motivation? Are you feeling overwhelmed by everything you have to do? You do have a lot on your plate right now. Are there commitments in your life that threaten to distract you from your goals? Do you have family needs to attend to? A boyfriend or girlfriend who wants more of your time? Are you juggling school and a job? School requires a significant investment of time, energy, and often money, and you can't afford to waste any of these. Part of your job as a student is to clear the path to your motivation. With this motivation brought out into the open, your success can follow right behind.

Let's begin by taking a deep breath and telling ourselves that, no matter what, these days in school are going to be good ones, full of promise and achievement. Whenever you're feeling overwhelmed, remind yourself that others, not much different from yourself, have managed to succeed in school, so why shouldn't you? One step toward success starts with this book. It's filled with thoughts, feelings, and advice from students just like yourself. We have gathered this information from all over the country and have organized it in a way to make it most useful for you. Think of it as a resource to turn to when you're looking for ideas about how to make your school experience a positive one.

## Self-esteem and Self-validation

A good place to begin our discussion is with the issue of self-esteem. Self-esteem is that part of you that determines how you feel about yourself. Do you value who you are? Do you feel that you're important? Do you blow up or minimize your accomplishments?

Low self-esteem is a widespread problem, and surprisingly, it affects many people for whom such a problem would seem unimaginable. A magazine cover model can suffer from serious low-esteem as can an extremely wealthy person who worries that people only like him for his money. Low self-esteem can be brought about by parents who are neglectful, with-holding of love and affection, or who are hypercriti-cal. Such parents, unfortunately, are to be found in every level of society.

How do you know if your self-esteem is in need of a boost? Ask yourself a few key questions.

1. How do you feel about coming into a room full of strangers?

2. Do you immediately see yourself as the least interesting/successful/worthwhile person in the room?

3. Does everybody seem better dressed, more so-cially confident, and better at mixing than you do?

Think about your goals and ambitions:

1. Do you go after the things that interest you?

2. Do you take a "why bother?" approach, knowing deep down that you screw up every-thing anyway?

Self-validation is an important issue as well. What does it mean to "validate" something? Well, think about it. You go to the mall and you have your park-ing ticket "validated" at one of the stores. That valida-tion is a way to prove that you were there being a good shopper, and your reward is free parking. When we use the term "validation" with regard to personal growth, we're referring to something similar to the validation of the parking ticket. We're talking about "proof" that you exist as a significant person in this world. Too many of us look to other people for that validation. This need to have others validate us can cause us to become needy individuals, always looking on the outside for something that we would be better off finding within.

Let's hear what your fellow students have to say on the issue of self-esteem and self-validation.

◙ **To me, it's the real core issue** of a person's life. You're not going to get ahead if you think of yourself as a toad. I have friends who think of themselves just like that. I have this one girlfriend—I'll call her Brenda—and she's amazing. She's smart, she's beautiful, she's got this incredible auburn hair that you could die for, but she thinks she's a toad. Why? Because her mother was always favoring her sister who wasn't nearly as pretty or smart or nice as Brenda was, and her mother felt she had to equalize things and be more loving to the one who "needed" it more. So Brenda wound up always feeling less deserving, less loved, less "getting." I don't compare to Brenda in terms of looks or smarts, but I have to say I do a lot better in life than she does because I leave her in the dust in the confidence department.

◙ **Some of us** are born to "withholding parents" and it's hard to make up for that. A piece of you is always looking for that approval and always feeling like you're not worthy of it. But you can get beyond that handicap. I have. It's taken a lot of work, but I think I've gotten to a point where my mother's critical voice is not the first thing I hear when I make a mistake.

◉ **My parents are good people.** They really care about me and my brother, have always made a really nice home for us, and gotten us everything we've needed and pretty much everything we've wanted. Sometimes, though, I think the lesson I got from them was that I'm only really validated by how much I've got: how many *things*. Like they've never really understood why I'd want to go into teaching young kids, which is what I think I want to do now. To them, that means never having enough money, so why bother?

◉ **My self-esteem really took a beating** from a lot of people who didn't know I had Attention Deficit Disorder (ADD). They thought I was just a pain-in-the-butt kid who couldn't settle down. No one ever treated me like I had any real chance for success.

◉ **I was abused as a child** and spent years abusing myself. My self-esteem died totally, but with a lot of good help, I got beyond it. Now I know what it's like to live with self-esteem and I'll never give that up.

## Searching for Success

For most of us, success and self-esteem go hand in hand. It's hard to feel good about ourselves if we haven't met our standard of success. As we grow older and realize that we may not meet the goals we set for ourselves, some of which may have been impossible, we will, if we're psychologically healthy, make adjustments to our concept of success. We may draw on the fact that even though we have not been the world's greatest whatever it was we wanted to be, we are wonderful fathers or mothers or husbands or wives. We draw satisfaction from our accomplishments wherever they come. In our youth, however, many of us are harsh taskmasters who drive ourselves to what we hope will be success and who berate ourselves if we fall short.

If your standard of success is placed too high, you may never get to know what self-esteem feels like. This can be even more of a problem if we allow others to define success for us. Maybe your parents think that the only way to be successful is to be a doctor or a lawyer. Maybe their definition of success is somebody who makes $50,000 a year or more. A lot of women grow up in families where the benchmark of success is how well you marry. Is your husband a doctor or a lawyer and does he make over $50,000 a year? If not, the message is that you haven't married well and you've screwed up.

You can listen to what people have to say—maybe you feel that you don't have a choice—but in the end, your definition of success has to be *your* definition of success. You're the one who's going to be living with it. If you just look at the medical field alone, you'll find that too many doctors went to medical school for the wrong reasons, either because their parents wanted them to or because they thought they could get rich that way. People who go into a field like medicine for reasons like that are likely to get burned out, missing the deeper significance of the work, or are likely to fall short of being really fine physicians as they lack the deep commitment that this demanding profession requires.

Let's hear what some of your fellow students have to say on the subject of success and what it's all about.

◉ **I love my Dad**, but he was always pushing us to the limits. I mean, he was out there coaching us in everything—soccer, basketball, baseball—but if my brother or I ever screwed up in a game, we'd have to go through this whole talk examining in detail what went wrong. It wasn't enough that we were two of the better athletes in our high school. We always had to be the best, all the time, which left us feeling like we were never the best any of the time.

◉ **I think success is about knowing** what you want and going after it. That doesn't mean that you're always going to get it, and it doesn't mean that it's not going to hurt when you don't get it. What it means is that you're doing something—going after your goals—without a lot of conflict to slow you down and muck you up.

◉ **To be successful**, it helps to have a definition of success or a model of a person whom you think is really successful. For me, that person is my grandmother. She raised me and my brother and our two cousins. She never made any real money, but there was always food on the table and a roof over our heads. She showed us love, all the time, and when people needed something, she was there. I can't think of anybody more successful as a human being than Grandma.

◙ **Success is tricky.** You know that old saying, "Watch out what you wish for because you might get it!" I think there's a lot of meaning in that saying. I look at some people and it seems their success is more of a curse than a blessing.

◙ **There's this saying I like** about genius, how it's one-tenth inspiration and nine-tenths perspiration. I think you can say something similar about success. It's one-tenth luck and maybe two tenths talent, and the rest is plain hard work.

# Positive Thinking

A positive outlook on life immeasurably enriches success, self-validation, and self-esteem. People who have a more negative orientation can achieve success, too, but they have to work harder. Positive thinking is like rich soil; you can grow almost anything in it.

◙ **My sister Gail and I** couldn't be less alike. She's the original glass half-empty type while I'm glass half-full all the way. The two of us could go into a doughnut shop and while I'm carrying on about the custard and the chocolate icing, she's going on about how the holes have gotten bigger! She can really drive you crazy.

🔲 **It's one small step** from negative thinking to self-fulfilling prophecies. You know what that's like. You're standing at the foul line, going for three points to win the game, and you're telling yourself how you're not going to make it. Sure enough, you miss the first basket. The second basket comes along and you're saying, "If I were any good, I would've made the first basket." There goes the second basket. On your third try, you're saying to yourself, "You missed two baskets, silly. You really think you can make the third?" It's like the opposite of visualization where if you see yourself making the basket, you *do* make the basket. Here you see yourself missing and you *do* miss.

🔲 **I learned the secret** of positive self-thinking from my grandfather who lived with us when I was little. If my brothers and sisters or I were having trouble with something, like learning a piano piece let's say, or trying to remember sines and cosines for a math test, Gramps would say, "You can do it. I know you can do it. So do it!" I still hear those words today when I'm doing something hard. When I took my SATs, for instance, I played Gramps' words in my head. "You can do it. I know you can do it. So do it!" It helped a lot.

🔲 **There's a lot of negativity** just in the atmosphere. Everyone's stressed out about the world, about the economy, all of that. I try to stay connected to positive people. Hanging out with worriers and people who only see gloom and doom isn't good for my health.

▣ **There's a Buddhist belief** that you should look for the gift in whatever you do. You get into a fender-bender: major aggravation. What's the gift? You didn't die or kill anyone. You fail a test: aggravation. What's the gift? You sit down with your teacher to try to figure out what went wrong, and you and he get to know each other a little better. When you start to think this way—that there's a gift to be found in every situation—it creates a feeling of hope that can be very powerful.

---

### Positive Self-talk

One of the most effective ways of combating negative feelings is with a tool called *positive self-talk*. Imagine a coach giving a pep talk. That's what you're doing for yourself.

✳ When I'm feeling down, I use positive self-talk to boost myself up. I say nice things to myself like, "You're a good person. You can do it. You can get beyond this." At first, I felt a little dumb doing this, but it didn't take long for me to get used to it and then I started to see how good it was for me. I didn't grow up with a lot of people telling me how wonderful I was, so I had to learn to do it for myself.

---

* I can't think of a reason *not* to use positive self-talk. You might as well be your own best friend. There are enough people out there waiting for you to fall on your face.

* My mom went to this workshop and she taught me this technique that's sort of like positive self-talk but, in a way, it goes beyond it. It's what you call out if things get really bad, like the heavy artillery. Like at the moment, I'm over my head in debt, and if I start obsessing about it like what will I do if the alternator on my car blows, I'll just say to myself, *"Stop Thought."* That's the little trick that my mother brought back from the workshop and it really works. It's like this red flag that you hold up in your head. Sure, it's artificial, but so what? It does the trick.

# The Seven Guiding Principles

As you go through this book, you will be reading tips on everything from test-taking to listening skills to stress management and, well, a whole lot more. But the nuts-and-bolts advice that fills this book needs to be placed in the context of broader, more sweeping principles. These Seven Principles are designed to help you, as a student, determine what you value most in your life.

Once you've read through these principles, it is important to do what you can to keep them in your head. Try putting them on an index card that you carry in your wallet or your bag. If you want, turn them into a rhyme or a song and chant them at quiet times or once a day, or in the morning or before you go to sleep. The goal is to somehow internalize them so that they will be with you always and you can draw on them whenever you need to. Remember: you want to get this part of your life right. Maybe everything hasn't gone the way you would have liked it to in the past, but this is the present now—and the future—and with thought and self-examination, you can use this time of your life to become what you want to become.

## Principle #1: Listen Up

*Do you hear what I'm saying?*
*Are you listening to me?*
*You never listen!*

Do any of the above sound familiar? Do you get a lot of that from your parents and maybe even your teachers? We wouldn't be surprised. Not listening may be a habit you picked up in adolescence when it is common behavior to screen out words and voices you don't wish to hear. Today, everywhere you look, the adolescent experience is provided with "escape routes" in the form of television, video games, and computers: our technologically advanced society has made it so easy *not* to hear.

But here's a newsflash: it's time to start listening!

In truth, listening is something that most people—adolescents and adults—take for granted. To many of us, listening seems like a passive behavior. It just "sort of happens." In fact, it doesn't just sort of happen. Listening—if you go about it correctly—should be active in nature. Good listeners are involved and engaged listeners. And to be a good student—that is, a successful student—it is absolutely necessary to become a good listener.

Later in the book, we will have a whole chapter that includes specific tips on listening. As a guiding principle, however, we want to take this moment to stress the vital importance of listening to what others have to say. Many of us are so overwhelmed by the demands and stresses of school, work, and whatever else is going on in our personal lives that we look for relief by drowning out our surrounding environment. In fact, such actions intensify stress. You can get more stress relief by keeping open the lines of communication and enjoying your contact with other people.

*Did you hear what we said?*

## Principle #2: Thinking Outside the Box

Life will be a lot more interesting if you avoid the trap of conventional, unimaginative, stereotyped thinking. Let's call it "stale thinking." It's thinking that's been around too long, that perhaps is passed down to you by family members or spread to you by friends. It's the kind of thinking that categorizes people into groups. This kind of stereotypical thinking is usually 100 percent wrong and can get you into a whole lot of trouble. Worst of all, it can deprive you of really meaningful opportunities that you could be enjoying with others.

Stereotypical thinking can also infect the way you view the subject matters you are asked to study. "Math is for men." "Art is for women." "Who cares about Shakespeare?" "Why do I need to know this? I'm never going to use it." These are all examples of stale thinking, and stale thinking—like stale doughnuts—deserves to go right into the trash. Get rid of it, and put new, fresh, open, and adventurous thinking in its place.

## Principle #3: Take Time to Figure Out What You Find Most Satisfying

There are very few people in this world who don't carry around at least a few bad associations with school. Maybe when you were little you had a teacher who criticized you for drawing outside the lines. Maybe you had a teacher who only called on the boys, leaving the girls to feel like they didn't count for anything. Did you have a good-hearted teacher who was deadly dull? Yep, we all did! But these negative associations with school should not set the tone for your current experiences.

School can be one of the most exciting, fulfilling, feel-good places in the world. Ask anyone who's graduated, who's out there in a desk job, dealing with stuff eight hours a day, and you'll see how they look back at school now. School is meant to be a time when students are engaged in the act of self-discovery, particularly in college. The opportunity to have such a time in your life is a great luxury and you need to savor it. You need to hit your stride so that each day in school is a day that you feel a little more alive and a little more complete as a human being, nothing less.

Mihaly Cziksentmihalyi, Ph.D., Professor of Psychology at the Drucker School of Management at Clermont Graduate University, wrote an important book called *Flow: The Psychology of Optimal Experience* (Harper Collins, 1991) in which he presented an interesting study he conducted with a test group of adolescents. He gave each of them a beeper that went off eight times a day over the course of one week each year. Every time the beepers signaled, the test subjects would report in about what they were doing and how they were feeling about it. Among other things, Dr. Cziksentmihalyi found that when people are involved in an activity they enjoy, they develop a sense of *flow*, a great feeling of energy that makes them want to continue doing what they're doing and return to it whenever possible.

In Chapter 2, we will offer a tool and a technique to help you figure out which activities give you that special sense of flow. We will help you assess how you spend your time and how you feel about what you're doing. We will take you through your day—

before, after, and during school—and we'll analyze where you feel most and least satisfied. This kind of honest assessment is a critical step you need to take before moving on to Principle #4.

## Principle #4: Create Time for the Things You Care About

The idea of shifting your time and energies to make room for the things you most enjoy might not seem like an option while you're a student, but you'd be surprised. As we said above, this may actually be one of the more flexible times of your life—during your college years, particularly—and if you use some of that thinking-outside-the-box approach, you'll see how you can manipulate your time.

Suppose, for instance, that you're the sort of person who can only really get started in the morning after you've had a half hour of quiet time to sit, read the paper, and sip your coffee. Or maybe what's really important to you right now is the daily exercise regimen you've established, and you know that the only time you can get it done without interruptions is first thing in the morning before you leave for school. One of your jobs might be to walk the family dog, but maybe you can switch that morning job with your sister who does the dishes after dinner. Yes, we understand that you're not crazy about doing dishes—who is?—but what's the most important consideration here? Isn't it that you get that morning time you need so badly? Maybe you don't even need to work out any kind of a trade. Maybe all you have to do is set your alarm clock a half hour earlier and wrest yourself out of that warm, cozy bed.

With regard to school, you may discover that the best way to stay on top of your work is to deal with it as soon as it's assigned. That may mean working for an hour or two on a Friday night to get it out of the way before the weekend sets in. Or maybe you do better when you let things sit a while and have deadlines breathing down on you. Whatever works. You're the judge. The key is to begin thinking about how you can best meet your needs because when your needs are met, you have a better chance of spending time with those things you really care about.

## Principle #5: Learn to Enjoy What's in Front of You

One of the students quoted earlier mentioned the Buddhist concept of "finding the gift" in any and all situations. We'd like to direct your attention to another Buddhist practice called "mindfulness" that teaches the value of focusing on what is beautiful in the here and now. Mindfulness urges us to live in the moment. Learning to develop this kind of vision is a huge help in clearing away the clutter of our lives.

How often have you found yourself thinking about everything other than what you are doing? You may be sitting in class and your mind is wandering to the bad wheezy sound that you heard coming out of your car that morning, or an argument that you had with a friend or a million other things. Think about what it would be like to really focus in on the moment and to get the most out of your class. Your teacher and your fellow students have a lot of worthwhile things to say. *You* have a lot of worthwhile things to say, too, and your active participation will go a long way toward making that class a better experience for everyone.

This practice of mindfulness can and should be used outside of school, too. When you're driving home, for instance, instead of thinking about that argument or the weird sound in your car or a school project coming due, think instead about how beautiful the light in the sky looks at that very moment or how peaceful the sound of the rain on your rooftop is.

## Principle #6: Learn to be Flexible

There is no such thing as a day that goes exactly according to plan. You have to learn to roll with the punches and the bumps and the trap doors that are always opening up all over the place. School involves a lot of routine, but things always come along to interrupt those routines such as your absence, a teacher's absence, bad weather, a special guest in the classroom, you name it.

If you think of yourself as a kind of machine that is out there every day getting the work done (but of course you are much more than that!), then flexibility is the lubricant that keeps your gears in working order. Flexibility makes stress fall away and also softens the hard edges that can cause damage in one's interactions with others. Flexibility will keep you from turning into a tight rubber band, ready to snap. Flexibility is like the elastic that allows you to retain your shape.

## Principle #7: Prioritize

Once you know what you have to do—and what you *love* to do—it's time to prioritize and get rid of all the unnecessary, energy-sapping tasks that you dread. You'll be shocked by just how much choice you have when it comes to investing your time and energy. Remember to keep track of what you actually do with your time. Ask yourself:

* What tasks and responsibilities do I need to take care of personally that absolutely no one else can do? For example, do I need to go food shopping at the end of the day or should I get together with some fellow students to tackle that subject matter that seems so hard?

* Which of my responsibilities can I put off for the moment, to be dealt with later with no harm done? What can I delay and what absolutely has to be done now?

* What am I doing that someone else could be doing for me? Could I ask my mother or my sister or my friend to take my dress to the cleaner? Could my brother deal with the snow tires?

* Is there something I can do differently so that I can make my life a little easier? For instance, could I order my boyfriend's birthday present over the Internet instead of going to the mall to buy it?

Embodying these Seven Guiding Principles and letting them show you the way is not something that happens overnight. Some people take months, even years, before they can internalize them, and even then, most have to be careful not to let old habits creep back into place. But we are not putting these principles forth as way to create even more pressure for you. As time goes on, these principles will, hopefully, come to feel like second nature. When you fully understand them and learn to live by them, you can use them in the work situations that will follow your school experience, and you will come to appreciate and enjoy a quality of life you might never have experienced otherwise.

## Chapter 2

# Staying on Track

**G**enerally, when people ask, "How are you doing?" most of us answer, "Fine, thanks." We assume that there is little real interest in what's good or bad about our day. Such exchanges are seen by most of us as just a way of being polite. But as the day goes on and we experience that same exchange over and over again—"How are you doing?" "Fine, thanks"—the details of our lives often get blurred or even lost along the way. By the end of the day, we may find ourselves not even sure whether things actually were fine, thank you.

In this chapter, we want to break away from all that. We are going to ask you to give serious thought to how you actually spend your day, moment to moment and hour to hour. The best way to begin doing this is to keep a record of where all your time goes.

Most of us spend at least 16 out of every 24 hours a day awake and active. In those waking hours, some of what we do might leave us feeling great. We may have been lucky enough to have been involved with activities that energize us and make us happy, giving us that sense of "flow" that we cited in the first chapter. But, unfortunately, most of us have to spend some of our time, or even a lot of our time, doing things that we would rather not be doing, things that are boring or unpleasant or simply routine.

The truth is that most of us don't have all that much choice when it comes to doing what we have to do. We need to attend to the humdrum duties of life such as walking the dog, doing the laundry, cleaning up after ourselves, and so on. But it is our belief that most of us can actually exert more control over our lives than we think we can. The key is to make a study of how we actually use our time and to keep track of how we feel about the ways in which we use our time. Once we've observed our patterns, then we can begin to think about making some changes.

Think about how you're spending your time. Here you are, a student, but maybe you're doing double-duty, too, like holding down a job. If you're an older student, you might have a husband or a wife and kids to take care of. This book is very focused on helping you deal with the demands being made on you, and the way to start is by looking at how you're using your time. Let's hear from your fellow students on how they're coping.

◙ **Sometimes I just feel overwhelmed** by school. To put it bluntly, I'm not the world's greatest student. My brother, who's a year older than me, is like Mister Perfect when it comes to school. He doesn't even have to study, and he comes up with A's every time. I, on the other hand, have to work overtime just to keep my head above water.

◙ **I feel like I'm a juggler** and not a very good juggler, either. I drop the ball a lot. I'm okay if things are going okay, but if the least little thing happens, I jump the track. Like the alternator on my car broke down last week. I missed a day of school, and I got behind and, and well, it just took a lot to get me up to speed again.

◙ **I'm the kind of person** who always takes on too much. I have a terrible time just saying "no." I get involved in everything at school—I'm in lots of clubs and I play volleyball and I do this inner-city tutoring project—and then I find myself up against the wall, with two days' worth of course reading I have to do and I start to panic.

◙ **Sometimes I get so overloaded with work** and pressure and deadlines that I just go into a total turn-off mode. I can't look at a book or think about writing a paper or do anything more than just lie in bed and watch television. Then I feel worse and worse, incredibly guilty, and I eat a whole container of ice cream and I hate myself.

◉ **I spend too much of every day** worrying. Instead of focusing in on what I have to do, I worry about what I have to do and whether I'm good enough to do it. I swear, I do such a number on myself sometimes.

 Keeping Track

Imagine yourself in biology. You're dissecting a fetal pig. You're the scientist; the pig is the specimen. Got the picture? Now let's adjust it a little. You're still the scientist but the fetal pig is gone. You are in its place. You have become the specimen. For the rest of this chapter, we want you to wear two hats: The Scientist Hat and The Specimen Hat. Do you think you can do that? Hopefully you can, because the idea here is for you to *examine your life*. We want you to develop a real awareness as to how you spend your time so that you can make sure you're working up to your potential, and that you're getting pleasure and satisfaction in the bargain.

Your assignment is to examine your day, start to finish. Train that scientific eye on yourself and get the answers to these questions:

Where do you go on any given day?

What do you do?

How do you feel when you're doing what you're doing?

The pages that follow in this chapter will make up a scientific log of sorts. To help you in your research, we will show you how to create a chart by which you can keep systematic track of your day. The headings of the chart will look like this:

* Start/Stop/Total

* Activity

* Feelings

* Efficiency

* What's My Role?

You can easily create this chart in a notebook that you can carry around with you throughout the day. The small spiral-bound type will fit into almost any coat or jacket pocket for easy access.

Ideally, you will be creating a record that reflects exactly what you've done with your time in the course of any given day. Your findings will become more significant if you stay with this record-keeping for a while, at least for a full week. That way, you will be able to see the difference between your work-week and your weekend, and the contrast can tell you a lot about how you regard your various activities.

At first, in the course of a busy day, you may find it difficult to grab the few minutes needed to log your activities. With classes to attend and projects to complete and all the demands that fill the rest of your life, finding the time to make notes about your feelings can, in and of itself, feel like a tall order. But the idea of this exercise is to make your life easier, not harder, so just do your best. Jot down your notes if you can while the experience is still fresh. Try to glance at your watch so you can make a mental note of the time you begin and end an activity. The jotting-down part can always come later.

So then, without further ado, here's how.

## Start/Stop/Total

Ready to take a good look at your day? Ready to feel proud of that time you spent helping your little brother with that homework? Ready to feel not-so-proud of those hours you wasted watching reality television?

In order for you to take stock of your day, you're going to have to be conscious of the clock, from the moment your alarm goes off in the morning until you close your eyes at night. Think about the many distinct activities that make up your day: getting to school; class time; lunch; afterschool activities; a job if you have one; coursework you do at home; household chores; exercise; and on and on. Each time you begin a new activity, jot down the "Start" time. Do the same when you finish that activity—note the "Stop" time—before you move on to your next activity. Don't neglect to factor in downtime like "hanging with friends " or whatever. As for the "Total Time Spent," don't worry about that until later. You don't need to burden yourself with adding, subtracting, and justifying yourself in the middle of a busy day. This is just straight numbers—10 minutes to walk the dog; 25 minutes on the bus to school; a half hour at lunch, and the like—and you can easily tally it all up at the end of the day.

▣ **This Start/Stop/Total exercise** is pretty cool. I can look at my whole day and see what I've gotten done and what I haven't gotten done. It made me feel like I've got more time available to me than I thought I did.

▣ **If you really follow the assignment** and do what you're supposed to do, it's kind of outrageous. Like, after four or five days, I realized that I was talking to my girlfriend for over an hour every day. I like talking to my girlfriend and she kind of expects it, but when I do the numbers, I can see that I really don't have the time for it right now. Or the money. It's a place where I think I can cut back. Like, we can talk on the phone maybe a half hour a day and I think that would work.

▣ **Doing this** got me to see some patterns. Like I realized I walk the dog 15 minutes a day and I exercise 45 minutes a day. So I said to myself, "Hey, genius, you could exercise by walking the dog!" I could save myself *hours* a week doing that and I could put those hours to good use somewhere else.

## Activity

Once you start filling in your Activity chart, you'll see how many different hats you wear in a single day. You'll see yourself as a student (*took Lit test*), as child (*drove Mom to the airport*), as friend (*going-away party for*

Sandy), as lover (*dinner at Julio's*), as employee (*cleaned out storeroom*), as neighbor (*picked up prescription for Mrs. Jackson*), and more. Your Activity entries will help you focus in on all these activities. In particular, they'll focus in on all your school activities since this is where you are spending the bulk of your time right now. You'll be able to see where you put your time relative to the subjects you are studying, and by the time you complete this activity, you'll get a record of how you *feel* about where you're putting your time with regard to these subjects.

When you're working on this log, we want you to keep in mind that this is not something you're going to be graded on. This is for your eyes and your eyes only. You are the sole contributor and the only one who will be reading this. The goal is to learn about yourself, how you spend your time, and how you feel during the course of the day.

◉ **It was interesting** because I realized that I was spending more time on subjects that I liked, like French and English, and less time on subjects I disliked, like math. That doesn't mean I should've been doing this, but that's what the record showed.

◉ **One thing that felt good** about doing this was seeing how much I manage to get done. School, working at the photo shop, making dinner for my father and brother, and so on. I'm not too bad if I do say so myself!

## Feelings

Soon after you've finished an activity, do your best to jot down your feelings about it. The closer you are to the activity, the truer the feelings will be and you will be less inclined to edit them, either consciously or unconsciously. It isn't important to write long, detailed notes at this point. A few well-chosen words will do just fine. A good way to begin is to think in terms of "feeling" words: are you happy, sad, angry, bored, worried? Next, try thinking in terms of opposites such as happy/sad, relaxed/tense, worried/optimistic, loving/angry, gentle/tough, energetic/tired, and interested/bored, and judging which of the two poles you feel closer to in each instance.

Your goal in this section is to gauge how much satisfaction you're getting out of your activities. Most of us have to do things that aren't exactly satisfying, but aspects of these activities can still bring us satisfaction. For instance, you may have to rake leaves/but you love the way a raked lawn looks. You might not feel like cooking tonight/but you're gratified by the expression on the face of the person for whom you've cooked. You may not feel like driving crosstown to return that suitcase with a broken lock to the store where you bought it/but on the way there you listen to an amazing radio program that has totally captivated your interest. As you can see, keeping a record of the feelings you experience during the day will help you identify the things that give you pleasure as compared to the things that bring you displeasure, and, if certain patterns emerge—you love drawing and working with computers, let's say—you may be pointed in a vocational direction that you feel could hold your interest over the long run, like computer-assisted graphic design.

Remember not to think too hard and too long when you write down your reactions. Your gut response is probably the most reliable. Again, keep in mind that this log is for your eyes only so don't worry about what others will think when you put down your honest reactions.

◉ **I enjoyed this part.** It reminded me of when I was a kid and I'd keep a diary and write down my feelings. When I'm running around a lot, just trying to get things done and to stay on top of it all, my feelings sometimes have to take a back seat. Doing this part of the log puts my feelings in the front seat, which is where they really belong.

## Efficiency

Think about your teachers. Some are more efficient than others, aren't they? Take Mrs. Tidy. She always remembers her handouts, knows where the pencils and paper are, and is clear on how to work the overhead. Is she your best teacher? Not necessarily. Maybe you favor Mr. Bumble, your history teacher, who forgets stuff every day but who can make the Battle of Gettysburg simply come alive.

Efficiency is not the most important thing in the world. As we've described above, we have all known people who are incredibly efficient and who bore us to tears. But it does count for something, particularly so in the life of a student. You don't need to be told that you've got a lot to keep on top of. Your coursework alone requires careful use of your time if you want to do your best. When you get out into the world, efficiency counts for something, too. So it's something to keep in mind and take note of, but not necessarily something to obsess about unless your log tells you that your inefficiency is costing you a lot.

When addressing this subject in your log, keep in mind that there may be instances where efficiency really doesn't apply very much at all. For example, if you are looking at the time of day when you take a bath, efficiency doesn't necessarily enter into that picture. It might be more "efficient" for you to take your bath in four minutes. On the other hand, it might be better for you, in the bigger picture, to take a half hour with your bath, just lying and soaking away the stress of the day. You be the judge. And if you determine that efficiency does not apply to a given task, simply write N/A (not applicable) in your log. Otherwise, make an effort to rate your efficiency in any given activity on a 1-to-5 scale.

▣ **After keeping the log**, I saw how inefficient I was in some areas of my life. Like shopping. I had to run out every other day to get stuff like shampoo or milk or cat food. If I was more efficient, I could make one or even two trips to the store a week.

## What's My Role?

As we've suggested, over the course of 24 hours, you, like most other people in the world, play a variety of roles. Not only are you student but also maybe you're a dancer or a sales clerk or a brother or a sister or a child or a grandchild or a political activist or a Little League coach or an emergency medical volunteer or . . .well, you get the idea. It is useful to think about which of these roles you most enjoy and which of them suit you best. For instance, even though you're a student, maybe you enact the role of a teacher now and then when you help a classmate understand something that you've been able to nail down. Think about the roles you play and over the course of a given week, compile a list of them somewhere in the back of your notebook or pad. As you fill in your log, figure out which roles you've been playing for which activity, but don't feel that you have to write these down so close to the time of the activity. This category and the next—End-of-Day Analysis—can be filled in when you find some quiet time for reflection.

|  | Activity #1 | Activity #2 | Activity #3 |
|---|---|---|---|
| Start<br>Stop<br>Total |  |  |  |
| Feelings |  |  |  |
| Efficiency |  |  |  |
| What's My Role? |  |  |  |

## End-of-Day Analysis

Now for the payoff! The very last thing you do each day, just before you turn out the lights, is to analyze your log. This is your opportunity to learn something about yourself, and believe it or not, for many people, the results are genuinely surprising. Follow the steps below:

1. Begin by totaling the first column, Start/Stop/Total. Add up the total for each activity and note it.

2. Review what you've written in the Activity column and read across the row to What's My Role? Think about what your role has been in each activity and note it in the appropriate place.

3. When you've filled in the entire What's My Role? column, check back to the Feelings column and think about which roles you found most pleasurable or satisfying. Note as well those activities that you found least pleasurable or satisfying. Give yourself time to think about how you might rearrange your life to maximize your time spent in the pleasurable roles and minimize the time spent in those roles you do not enjoy.

4. Look back at your Start/Stop/Total column and match it up against the Feelings column. How much time did you spend doing things that offered you very little satisfaction? How much time did you get to spend doing the things you most love to do?

5. Think about what was most surprising in your log and make a note of it. Perhaps it was how much time you spent doing things that you genuinely do not enjoy. Or maybe—hopefully—it was the other way around. Maybe you're surprised by how much pleasure you took in learning some of the more scientific aspects of your coursework. Maybe you were surprised by how interested you were in reading that special poem.

6. Repeat this process every day for a week, each day with a new log. At the end of the week, go over all your notes, paying special attention to the End-of-the-Day Analysis. Give yourself ample time to think about what you are reading.

Again, the goal here is to reflect. Ultimately, you will want to find enough time in your life to do more of what you love to do and less of what you don't like to do. In order to achieve that goal, you will need to keep track of the Seven Guiding Principles:

1. Become an active listener

2. Think outside of the box

3. Take time to figure out what you find most satisfying

4. Create time for the things you care about

5. Learn to enjoy what is in front of you

6. Learn to be flexible

7. Prioritize

Keeping a log and being mindful of the Seven Guiding Principles is only one step toward making the most of your life as a student. The next chapter will introduce you to the very important work of setting and achieving goals.

## Chapter 3

# THE GOAL ZONE

What do you want to be when you grow up?
*A fireman.*
*A ballerina.*
*A racing car driver.*
*The President of the United States.*

**D**reaming can be a wonderful thing. Dreams fuel our achievements and occupy our interests in ways that are, for the most part, constructive. As a child, maybe you went out to the skating rink at five in the morning, hoping you would be the next Olympic sensation. Perhaps you practiced the piano, picturing yourself on some grand concert stage. Or maybe you were one of those kids who fantasized about the weightlessness you would experience when serving as an astronaut.

The fact that these dreams may not be fulfilled is hardly a surprise. While these fantasies can capture our imagination for long periods of time, eventually, we may decide to exchange them for objectives that feel more attainable. We might decide that it would be just as wonderful to become a kindergarten teacher or civil engineer. We look around us at the adult world and see that other factors enter into the decision-making process of our lives such as security, having a family, and owning a home. Our dreams change and we move closer to reality.

What we have just described is the most normal human process imaginable. We are all finding our way through life, which can be an enormously complicated task. The world of the past—when Father went to work for a big corporation and stayed there for 50 years and Mother kept the home fires going—has been supplanted by a far more changeable world where people need to hone the skills that will allow them to adapt to a highly competitive global economy and a far more fragmented social structure.

This is the world that you are entering and it can be a little scary. Chances are, your family and friends have already started to talk to you about what your "plans" are and you may not have any fast answers for them. You may not know if you're going to be a dentist or a data processor, a florist or a fisherman, a cook or a court reporter. If you're in this situation, we have two words for you: *Don't panic.* You are not alone. Being unsure about your next step in life is a common symptom of the human condition and is entirely appropriate to those who are currently enrolled in school. In fact, it is understood that school is the place where you're meant to be doing a great deal of thinking about your future. It is a period of growth and development, so don't make it harder by layering panic on top of it.

Right now, you are in the business of turning your dreams into goals, goals that you can actually achieve. Therefore, we have made goal-setting the focus of this chapter. We will be discussing ways to set goals and to realize them. The fact that you're sitting here right now reading these words means that you know something about goal-setting, even if you're not entirely aware of it. Your goal was to further your education, and here you are, doing just that, which puts you leagues ahead of those individuals who haven't got a clue about their future or where they're headed. But an important thing to know about goals is that they have a way of changing. That means that you have to continually examine the process of goal-setting to make sure that you are headed where you really want to go.

For most people, goals are closely connected to a concept of success. We touched on the issue of success in the first chapter, but we'd like to briefly revisit it here.

## The Fundamentals of Success

Success does not mean the same thing to all people. There isn't just one way to be successful. Let's look at some of the meanings that success has for your fellow students.

▣ **Success means money**. End of story. Look around you. The people who have money have good lives. You don't need a road map to figure that one out.

▣ **To me, there's a lot more to success** than making money. I mean, there are plenty of rich people and plenty of not so rich people who are looking for something they can never buy with a credit card. To me, success means whether you're a good human being or not.

▣ **You don't have to be a genius** to be successful. The best route to success is to know what you want and to go after it. So many people are conflicted about what they want that they can never hope to achieve it.

▣ **I was raised by my grandparents** who owned a seafood restaurant. They did really well, but they worked their buns off. They'd always tell me how you can't get ahead in this world unless you're willing to put in the hours. "There are no free rides," they'd say, and what determines success the most is learning and practicing and getting good at something. For the most part, it's not about magic.

▣ **My dad always used to tell us** that success isn't about the good times. Success is about how you get through the bad times. Everybody has bad times, at some time or another, and if you cave when the going gets tough, your so-called success is going to go up in smoke.

▣ **I had this amazing soccer coach**, Coach Budega, from Hungary, and unlike a lot of other people in sports, was a real progressive thinker. He used to tell us that almost anybody could be successful if they could figure out what their gift was. He said we were all born with some kind of gift, some special thing that maybe we hadn't even discovered yet. Maybe we were fast or strong or musical or mathematical or exceptionally kind and patient or funny or incredibly dependable. The trap was thinking of yourself as "ordinary." That's what killed your shot at success.

## Success Do's and Don'ts

You all know the expression, "Shooting yourself in the foot," don't you? It means finding ways to undermine your success. Now, given the fact that success seems to be such a sweet thing, why on earth would people want to jeopardize their chances for it? Well, for one thing, they may have very conflicted feelings about success. They may, for instance, have gotten some mixed messages about success growing up. For example, in certain cultures, it is the hope of the parents that their children will surpass them in terms of material success. In other cultures, however, it is frowned on for a child to surpass his parents. If you come out of this kind of culture, you might be avoiding success for this reason. In a whole other scenario, perhaps you have a fear of success because, deep down, you feel a certain sense of inadequacy that you've never dealt with and you're afraid that if you appear to be successful, you might somehow be "exposed." We invite you to give some thought to the ways that you have been taught about success. It is useful to judge whether we encourage success in ourselves or discourage it. Let's hear what your fellow students have to say on the subject.

## Procrastination

A big "don't," and one that plagues a lot of people.

◉ **I've never been a great student.** I was the kid who always took the last seat in the row, trying to hide behind someone. It's just not the way I saw myself. I always had a hard time concentrating and focusing in on my work. If I could put off till tomorrow what I could do today, that would be my choice. Better yet until next week. It's what you call procrastination and it's one of the hardest habits to break.

◉ **Yeah, I'm a procrastinator.** I admit it. But I've learned some ways of dealing with it. In high school, we had this school psychologist; he was a cool guy. He taught me some good stuff about procrastination. He gave me these techniques that he called "procrastination-busters." If you're really dreading something, like studying for a huge exam or whatever, you can find some little bitty part of the job to start with. Maybe it's sharpening pencils. Maybe organizing file cards, I don't know, whatever. You've just got to learn not to sit there and be paralyzed.

## Perfectionism

Another big "don't." Not quite as widespread as procrastination, but just as counterproductive.

◉ **The thing I have to overcome** if I'm going to be successful is my perfectionism. It's crazy, and it runs in the family. My father is like Mr. Perfectionist. He's such a control freak, it's incredible (I think perfectionism and being a control freak go hand-in-hand). If you're going to a wedding, your shoes have to be polished so they look like mirrors. If you wash the car, then you've got to polish it and the hood has to be like a mirror. I don't know what it is with my father and mirrors. Like I said, I'm that way, too, though not half as bad. At least I know that perfectionism is not a good thing. Feeling like you have to be perfect in order to be successful can kill off motivation, and motivation is what actually breeds success.

◉ **I took this psychology course** in high school where we learned all about motivation, and you've got to understand motivation to understand the trap of perfectionism. There are two types: *extrinsic* and *intrinsic*. Extrinsic motivation is when you get it from the outside. Your father offers to buy you a car if you get all A's on your report card. That's extrinsic. Intrinsic motivation is when you get it from the inside. You get all A's on your report card because you know how good it feels to do the best you can. Intrinsic is usually more long-lasting and effective than extrinsic. When the motivation is intrinsic, you're less likely to do a perfectionist number on yourself.

◙ **Perfectionism is just a way** to punish yourself. None of us is perfect. You could be the world's best golfer and still slice it into the rough. You could be a gorgeous movie star and wake up with a pimple on your nose. The very idea of perfection is, when you think about it, anti-life.

◙ **I'm a nationally ranked** junior tennis player, and having been a serious athlete for a long time now, I've had my share of success and my share of disappointment. At first, the disappointment was hard to cope with. When I lost a game, I had to learn not to beat up on myself. I really didn't help my chances of success by wearing myself out with self-criticism. Instead, I told myself that everyone makes mistakes. Everyone goes through periods where they're not lucky and nothing's happening for them. Keeping up good feelings about yourself will make all the difference in getting through the tough stuff.

## Game Plans

Now here's a definite "do." A good game plan will make your life a lot easier.

◙ **If you're going to try** to be successful in this life, you'll need a game plan. A game plan helps you reach your goal. Trying to get where you want to go without a game plan is like going on a car trip without a road map.

◙ **My parents** own their own business. They have three laundromats. They're always telling me that if you're going to be in your own business, the important thing is to have a sense of where you're going. That's what a business plan is for: it's the blueprint to get you from here to there. It tells you what kind of profit you can expect to see and what you have to spend to reach your goal. My dad says I should think of myself as a business, but instead of making a business plan, I should make a game plan that will tell me where I can expect to be in one year, in two years, in five years, maybe even in 10 years.

◙ **As a student**, the game plan you figure out will help you determine where you're going to get your tuition money, where you're going to find a quiet place to study, how you can balance your life as a student with a job, and so on. It's important.

## Self-esteem

Developing positive self-esteem is a definite "do."

◙ **The real trump card** when it comes to playing the game of life is self-esteem. It's hard to have success without it. You could even be materially successful, but with low self-esteem, you will continue to feel small and empty inside.

◙ **I've learned to express my goals** in positive language. Now that may seem like a little thing, but it's not. I've always struggled with my weight, and so losing weight has always been a goal for me. I used to tell myself, "OK, you're not going to screw up another diet. This time you'll get it right for a change." Well, that kind of language was a constant reminder of how I'd failed over the years. Then my counselor taught me to use more positive language, so now I say things like, "You'll lose five pounds this month because you really know how to do it, kid." I form an alliance with myself and that feels so much better.

◉ **Fear of failure** and fear of success are flip sides of the same coin. Everyone fails but failure isn't the end of the world. It's just an end result of a specific action. Fear of success is mostly about the fear that you'll be exposed for the fraud you really are. That's really a self-esteem issue.

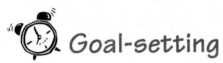 *Goal-setting*

By now, having gotten this far in the book, you should have some understanding of what constitutes success. You understand that success can be undermined by certain negative habits and behaviors like procrastination and perfectionism. You also understand that success can be promoted by certain good habits and behaviors like creating a game plan. Now's the time to look at the process of goal-setting, what it's all about, and what is the best way to go about it.

◉ **Not all goals** are created equal. Some goals are short-term: you can achieve them tomorrow or next week or a couple of months down the road. Passing a test, for instance, is a short-term goal. Long-term goals are the ones you work on over the long haul. Graduating from college is a good example of a long-term goal.

◉ **I try** to break down my goals, even my short-term ones, into smaller "goal-units" that I feel confident I can accomplish. My overall goal is to pass a course, but my smaller goal-units are to pass the quizzes and the tests and get my papers done.

◉ **Setting goals is fine.** Everybody should have goals, but if you're constantly setting up goals that you're going to fall short of, it's not such a great idea. Let's say you're 5'5" tall and your goal is to get drafted by the NBA. Okay, it may be possible, but how high do you want to set the bar for yourself?

◉ **Remember**, your goals are your own. Your father wants you to be a doctor and you want to be a bass player. Who wins? Your mother wants you to get married when you're 21 and you want to travel the world first. Who wins? I say *you* win, first and always.

◉ **Goal-setting never ends.** It's not like you get to the top of the heap and then you're finished-no more goals. There's always something more to aspire to. If your goal, for instance, has been to make a ton of money, and you have made a ton of money, maybe your new goal is to find great ways to give some of that money away.

## Types of Goals

Do you remember when you were a kid in Middle School and your health teacher taught you all about the food pyramid? Vegetables and grains were at the bottom, giving it a good foundation, and on the very top were things like ice cream and pepperoni sausage. Well, when thinking of your goals, it can be useful to visualize a kind of pyramid, too, that looks something like this:

* *Physical.* At the bottom of the pyramid, providing a strong foundation, is our health and physical well-being. It is difficult to achieve greatness on an empty stomach, although certainly some have.

* *Emotional.* Feeling good about ourselves is a wonderful aid in our pursuit of goals. It is so much easier to chalk up accomplishments when we aren't hearing a little voice in our heads telling us that we're fakes and fools.

* *Social.* Family, friends, and even pets are vital to help us really exist as successful people. No man is an island unto himself.

* *Mental.* We want to use our brains, our creativity, and our abilities to make valuable contributions to the world. Hopefully, our day-to-day work will be an outlet for our talents.

* *Spiritual.* The top of the pyramid suggests that there is a higher truth, some pattern that gives life meaning. You don't have to go to church to be on

a spiritual path, and many people never do ascend to this part of the pyramid, but those who do report a sense of satisfaction that is very, very special.

## Dealing with Disappointment

Goals are important, but the way you cope with *not* meeting your goals is just as important. We all fall short at various points in our lives, and our capacity to deal with disappointment will be one indicator of how successful we will be at navigating life.

▣ **You know that expression**, "I never promised you a rose garden?" Well, life is no rose garden. I found that out when I was a sophomore in high school. My whole life was basketball and I was really good. I thought I was going to have my choice of scholarships to college. Then, on Christmas Day, I was in a car accident. I broke a femur, my pelvis, and two vertebrae. That was the end of basketball for me, but I was lucky I survived altogether. The other thing that happened was that I became a really top student, which I probably never would have become if things hadn't turned out the way they did. So you see?

▣ **Disappointments stink**, but they can send you in whole new directions. They're like the switch on the railroad track. You thought the train was going to

Chicago and suddenly you're headed for Miami. But the weather's great in Miami, right?

◉ **My parents always taught us** that if we've been disappointed in something, it's important to look at the situation and to see what we did right and what we did wrong. Everything is a learning experience, they always told us. There's no such thing as failure. There's just good stuff and bad stuff, and we've got to learn from it all.

 Student Goals

We will be discussing your goals as a student in depth later in this book. But for now, it makes sense to give an overview of your goals as a student and how you can best work toward these goals. We polled your fellow students on the subject.

◉ **I want to be the best** I can be. This is *my* education. For the first time in my life, I'm claiming ownership of it. I'm not doing this to make someone else happy. I'm doing this for me.

◉ **I never miss a class.** I used to cut, but I gave it up. Bad habit, and teachers don't like it. Besides, there's too much to learn.

◉ **My older sister** Jen was a really top student and is a really great person. She's kind of my role model. She always says that being a student is a job, and that like any job, you've got to carry out certain basic duties. You've got to show up on time. You've got to do your homework. You've got to have basic respect for other people and listen to them. There's more, but that's a good start.

◙ **One of my goals as a student** is to really get used to being a student and to realize that, to some degree or another, all of us stay students throughout our lives. My mom is a paralegal, and she's always going off for refresher courses and weekend workshops and stuff. My grandfather was a pharmacist and he retired, but he didn't stop being a student, either. He took up jewelry-making out in Arizona, going to a class three times a week, and you should see the stuff he turns out now!

◙ **I've always been kind of shy** in the classroom, so one of my goals as a student is to speak up when I don't understand something. I ask a lot of questions but nobody seems to mind.

Now that we've looked at the mechanics of how goals and goal-setting work, let's turn our attention to some of the specific tools you need to achieve your goals, starting with the mind power that will help you get where you want to go.

## Chapter 4

# It's All in Your Mind

For some lucky people, school is a piece of cake. These gifted students sail through every course, pass their final exams with flying colors, toss off papers and other big projects, and drive everyone crazy with how easy they have it. Most students, however, tend to see school as more of a challenge. They work hard, marking time between vacations and fantasizing of a future when homework will be just a distant memory. Then there are those students for whom school becomes the stuff of nightmares. These students hide in the back of classrooms and can become physically sick with anxiety on test days. They do the minimum, squeaking by and looking for satisfaction elsewhere in their lives. To them, school is a dirty word.

If school has been an uphill challenge for you over the years, now may be the right time in your life to level the playing field. You're older now, and you're ready for different kinds of behavior. Think back to the last chapter. Do you remember what you read about goal-setting and motivation? By the way, remembering what you read is an educational objective called *retention*. It's important and it's something that you can learn how to do more effectively. As you may recall, the deepest form of motivation is the intrinsic sort, where the desire to achieve comes from within you, not from what your mother or your father or your grandfather has to say. If you've got that intrinsic motivation—and at this point in your life maybe you're starting to feel it kicking in—then you should be ready to commit the kind of energy, hours, money, and interest that a good education calls for. As you'll see, motivation is a force that can completely transform your school experience. Keep this formula in mind: School + Motivation = Achievement. With the right elements in place, there should be no stopping you now.

On the other hand, you may still be carrying around feelings of inadequacy from your earlier school experiences. Old wounds build up scar tissue that can interfere with your ability to see things with a new perspective in the here and now. We don't want that scar tissue to stand in the way of the potential you now have a chance to realize. This is the time to give school your best shot without any self-sabotaging behavior. To that end, we are going to use this chapter to focus in on the many productive ways that we can all learn to become better learners. All of us have marvelous reservoirs of brain power to tap into. That is not to say that we are all geniuses or that we're going to give some billionaire a run for his money, but if we understand how our minds work, then we can make the most of what we have. Tapping into our resources will allow us to perform better than we ever have before. So where to begin? Well, how about with the brain itself?

 ## The Big Brain

What weighs approximately three pounds and is made up of billions of cells so tiny that 30,000 of them would fit on the head of a pin? The answer, of course, is the human brain, that amazing organ that acts as the conductor for everything that goes on in our bodies. The brain tells our eyes, ears, nose, mouth, hands, and feet exactly what to do—laugh now! Cry! Blink! Snap your fingers! Wriggle your toes!—and it also regulates all of our basic life support systems like breathing and sleeping.

Those billions of tiny cells we mentioned above are called neurons. Neurons are activated by neurotransmitters, chemicals that move from one neuron to another, setting off electrical impulses. Whenever you learn a certain task or behavior, like tying your shoe or blowing on hot soup, you are doing so with the help of a specific group of neurons that are activated and that bring certain perceptions, memories, thoughts, and feelings into play.

The ability to store information is the key to the human being's success as a species. We can't swim like sharks, jump like kangaroos, or fly like eagles, but we can learn a lot. Pianists memorize entire concertos, athletes and dancers remember extremely complicated physical routines, mathematicians remember formulas, and actors remember lines. Students learn facts, formulas, and many other kinds of information. That is the job of the student and your neurons are ready to help you with the task.

A hard shell called the skull beautifully protects the human brain. The skull does a fine job of encasing the vulnerable brain, but even so, you really can't be too careful with the brain. Going skiing or motor biking without a helmet is a great way to damage your brain. Certain psychological responses to stressful situations, like anxiety or depression, can also impact on brain function, causing forgetfulness or other impairments. Fatigue will take its toll on brain function as well. As a student, you may have to burn the midnight oil before a big exam or a project comes due, but if you rely on such behavior routinely, you run the risk of burning yourself out. Rest, good nutrition, and regular exercise are vital ways to take care of that brain of yours.

# Intelligence

What can we say about intelligence? The real truth is that some of us may have more of it than others and some of us may have an easier time accessing what we have than others of us do. The interesting thing, however, is that there is no one kind of intelligence. More and more, researchers are rejecting the idea of a single kind of intelligence that can be measured on a quantifiable scale such as the IQ test. While it is true that certain kinds of intelligence can be assessed in this way, other forms of intelligence that are just as real do not lend themselves to such assessment. It is important for you, as a student, to understand that intelligence comes in different forms. In your earlier days as a student, the area of intelligence that was most representative of who you were might have been discounted, and your self-esteem and motivation might have been bruised or even stunted. We want to make sure that doesn't happen to you again.

Let's look back for a moment to 1979. That was the year that the eminent educator, Harold Gardner, Ph.D., of Harvard University, stood the academic world on its head with his Theory of Multiple Intelligences. Gardner's theory states that there are seven basic intelligences, which can be present in an individual in various degrees of strength (*Celebrating Multiple Intelligences*, 1994 & Armstrong, 1994). These seven basic intelligences are:

1. *Word Smart* (*Linguistic Intelligence*). The capacity to use words effectively, whether oral or written.

2. *Logic Smart* (*Logicomathematical Intelligence*). The ability to use numbers effectively and to reason well.

3. *Picture Smart (Spatial Intelligence)*. The capacity to see the visual–spatial world accurately.

4. *Body Smart (Bodily-Kinesthetic Intelligence)*. The ability to use the entire body as a means of expression, as well as to use the hands to make or alter things.

5. *Music Smart (Musical Intelligence)*. An aptitude for appreciating, creating, and /or expressing yourself through music.

6. *People Smart (Interpersonal Intelligence)*. The facility to know how to "read" other people and interact effectively with them.

7. *Self-Smart (Intrapersonal Intelligence)*. The capacity to see and know yourself well, and to reflect meaningfully on your experiences.

As we said above, all of us possess one or more of these kinds of intelligence, and each of these intelligences is just as important as the next. Recognizing this is vital to building up your all-important self-esteem.

◉ **From the time I was really little**—probably all the way back to kindergarten—I always thought of myself as the class moron. I couldn't add, I couldn't subtract; forget about dividing. But I was—and am—a really good dancer. I even thought about making a career of it if I hadn't damaged my tendons. I wish I'd known about this multiple intelligences theory earlier in my life so I could have felt better about myself.

◙ **Throughout my life**, I've had to deal with learning issues. I was a really late reader and that was hard. But I always had a lot of friends. People just seemed to gravitate to me and to trust me. I've channeled that talent into an ongoing involvement with student government. I'm really good at organizing things. So I guess that's what's meant by a social intelligence. I'm even thinking about trying to get into politics when I get out of school.

◙ **I used to be sent to the office** all the time because I'd sit in the back of the room and draw cartoons. I finally had a teacher in my sophomore year of high school—Mr. Dennis, an English teacher—who bothered to even look at my drawings. He thought they were really good and got me a spot on the school newspaper doing cartoons for them. It felt really good to be validated that way, to have somebody say I was good at something.

## Emotional Intelligence

You've probably heard something about emotional intelligence by now. It's been all over, in books (particularly the best seller *Emotional Intelligence* by Daniel Goleman), on the news, and in magazines. Emotional intelligence, which is closely linked to the intelligences listed above as People Smart and Self-Smart, is a form of social intelligence that allows you to "read" other people. According to researchers P. Salovey & J. D. Mayer in their article entitled "Emotional Intelligence" (*Imagination, Cognition, and Personality*, Vol. 9, 1990), there are five chief manifestations of emotional intelligence:

1. Self-awareness (the ability to monitor yourself and to recognize your feelings as you experience them).

2. Managing emotions (handling those feelings).

3. Motivating yourself (channeling your emotions in the service of a goal).

4. Empathy (sensitivity to the feelings and concerns of others).

5. Handling relationships (handling the emotions of others).

According to Daniel Goleman, "emotional intelligence . . . should become increasingly valued as a workplace asset in the years to come" (*Emotional Intelligence*, p. 160).

How emotionally intelligent are you feeling these days?

## Remember This . . .

One of the most important functions of the brain is to remember and retrieve information. Our brain reminds us to eat when we're hungry, to sleep when we're tired, to find our way home at night, to take our pills, and to study for a test. There is some data that our brains might be less attentive to—other people's birthdays perhaps or where we left our car in a crowded parking lot—but we can live with such shortcomings. As a student, however, failings of the memory can come with a pretty hefty price tag. Let's imagine, for instance, that you are taking a course on American history. Your final exam expects you to know some crucial dates such as the signing of the Declaration of Independence, Lincoln's assassination, or the bombing of Pearl Harbor. If you're the sort who has a hard time remembering what year the War of 1812 occurred, then these dates may well be your undoing and could cost you crucial points on your test score.

How, then, can one go about improving one's memory, turning it into a strength instead of a weakness? Let's hear how some of your fellow students have managed.

◙ **The best way to remember something?** Write it down. I always carry a little memo pad with me, the size of an index card. Everything I need to remember goes down on that pad. Everything. I look it over at least a couple of times every day. I've got friends who like to "keep things in their head." Hah! Very few people can do that; my friends sure can't. They're always calling me to find out what the homework is.

◙ **I drive to and from school** and there's always stuff I remember when I'm driving. So I got this little post-it thing for my dashboard with a built-in pencil. When I stop at a light, I write down what I need to remember. If I didn't do that, I'm sure all that stuff would be lost forever.

🔲 **I write things down, too,** but I've also discovered this other great trick. If I have something that I cannot, under any circumstances, forget—like calling my girlfriend on her birthday or paying a bill on a certain day or something like that—I'll leave a message for myself on my own phone machine. It's foolproof!

🔲 **Anytime I have to remember something** I say it five or six times in a row. *Pick up Aunt Lil at the airport at 7. Pick up Aunt Lil at the airport at 7. Pick up Aunt Lil at the airport at 7. Pick up Aunt Lil at the airport at 7. Pick up Aunt Lil at the airport at 7.* Or how about this? $\pi=3.14$. $\pi=3.14$. $\pi=3.14$. $\pi=3.14$. $\pi=3.14$. Of course, if anyone heard me muttering these things to myself, they'd probably think I was a complete mental case, but I'm sorry, that's the way I get things to stick in my mind.

🔲 **I've had teachers** who have really pushed mnemonics, which basically are these memory aids to hook your brain. The most famous one is probably HOMES, which is a way to memorize the five Great Lakes, with each letter of HOMES standing for one of the lakes (Huron, Ontario, Michigan, Erie, and Superior). I make up mnemonics like that all the time for myself. For instance, if I need five things in the store, I'll make up the mnemonic BEAMS for bread, eggs, apples, milk, salt. It's pretty effective, all right.

# The Care and Feeding of the Brain

The brain, like any other part of your body, benefits from tender loving care. We put lotion on our skin, have our aching backs and necks massaged, and splurge on manicures for our fingernails and pedicures for our toenails, but what exactly are we doing for our brains? Here are some tips from your fellow students suggesting some nice things you can do for your gray matter.

▣ **Make sure you get plenty of sleep** at night, and rest periodically during the day if you can. Instead of playing a video game, close your eyes. You'll recharge your brain better that way. Just think about how much your brain takes in on a daily basis, particularly in this high tech world where we're bombarded by images from the TV and the computer. Our brains are crying out for a little peace and quiet at the end of the day. So take a nap, do some meditation, and listen to some calming music with headphones on and a cool compress over your eyes. In other words, give your brain a break.

▣ **I like to do crossword puzzles**, acrostics, and hand-held video games. These are all ways I have of keeping my mind in shape. Some people might say I'm pushing my brain into overload, but I don't buy it. To me, it's like doing stretches.

▣ **We all know** how aerobic exercise is great for your heart and your lungs. Well, guess what? It's great for your brain, too, because it improves the oxygen flow so you can think a whole lot better.

◙ **Just the way a good balanced diet** helps your heart function and your kidneys and stuff, it's good for your brain, too. Take proteins, for instance. Proteins are what the neurotransmitters make building blocks out of, and the way to get these proteins is to make sure you're eating enough chicken, fish, meat, beans, seeds, and nuts.

◙ **You know what's really not great** for your brain? Overdosing on caffeine. I got into this thing where I was just chugging coffee and the cola all day long, and it wasn't good. Yeah, caffeine will "perk" you up for a while, but the brain knows better, and when it catches on to what you're trying to pull, it'll crash.

◙ **Alcohol is used to pickle stuff**, right? So why would you want to pickle your brain in alcohol?

 Think About It...

Most of us are lucky enough to be born with a functioning brain, but it's how we use that brain that is of crucial importance. Thinking is an acquired skill. People have to learn how to think, and some people may not be able to master that task until they reach maturity. Real thinking involves *critical thinking, logic, deductive* and *inductive reasoning,* and *creativity.* Let's have a look.

## Critical Thinking

As life's many complicated situations present themselves, we have to be able to look at them critically and make wise decisions. For instance, if we go to a party with someone, and that person gets drunk and then offers us a ride home, we have to look at that situation and judge it on its merits. Do we allow ourselves to be driven home by someone who gets behind the wheel after having downed six shots of bourbon? Of course not. We call a cab. This ability to analyze a situation and take appropriate action is called critical thinking and it depends on logic, reasoning, and the ability to separate fact from opinion.

▣ **Most people I know** have no idea what critical thinking is. I have this guy in my class who brought firecrackers into school in his backpack. Cut to the next scene: he's in jail. Don't you think he should have had the intelligence and the critical thinking ability to figure out that the combination of firecrackers and school is a really bad idea? You'd think so, but he didn't think. That was the problem.

## Logic

Training your mind to think in a disciplined kind of way can come in handy when you're dealing with life. Why not try on the role of the problem-solver, for instance? Problem-solvers are always going to be in demand, in any field, any job, any time, any place.

What will distinguish you as a problem-solver is the degree of logic you bring to your thinking. Logic is a disciplined, ordered form of thinking that is strong and that can support your actions. One type of logical thinking is called deductive reasoning. In deductive reasoning, the conclusion you come to is true because the underlying basis, also known as the premise, is also true. Consider this example:

Premise       Seatbelts have been proven to save lives.

Premise       John's car has four seatbelts.

Conclusion    Anyone traveling in John's car should use seatbelts.

Another type of logical thinking is called inductive reasoning. Here, the conclusion may often be true but you have to check to make sure. Consider this example of inductive reasoning:

Premise       Bob's grandfather is bald.

Premise       Baldness is often hereditary.

Conclusion    Bob will go bald.

Now there's a good likelihood that Bob's hair may thin, but inductive reasoning prevents us from reaching such a conclusion, doesn't it? After all, there are exceptions to the rule of heredity and Bob might be such an exception. For all we know, Bob is not even biologically related to his grandfather. Maybe he was adopted. The point is that you have to think before you reach a conclusion. That kind of thinking is exactly what the brain is there for.

Logical thinking also allows us to differentiate between fact and opinion. For example, claiming that meat is bad for you is an opinion. Although vegetarians might feel that eating meat is bad for you, you would not necessarily find any hard research to support such claims and, in fact, you might uncover research that would show that moderate meat-eating has certain nutritional benefits. Being able to distinguish between fact and opinion is a necessary skill to help you get through life as a responsible member of the community who votes and who feels that he or she has a role in the way society functions.

## Problem-Solving

There are two kinds of people in the world: those who think and those who depend on others to do their thinking for them. In our society, the vast majority of people fall into the second category. They are consumers of ideas, marketed to them by television, radio call-in shows, the Internet, and so forth. The rate at which this "unthinking" group is growing is alarming, particularly when you consider that many media outlets like newspapers and radio and television stations and magazines are all coming together under the umbrella of a small number of conglomerates. The ability of a few to control the thinking of many presents a real danger to democracy.

People who fall into the "thinking" group—who actually, genuinely know how to think and who realize that most problems are open to examination and creative solution—are always going to be in demand. Such people are problem-solvers who provide society with what it needs most: good ideas.

We spoke to students like yourself to see how they viewed the issue of problem-solving, and here are some of their responses.

◙ **You don't have to work** at some gigantic software company to be a problem-solver. You can be a problem-solver at the doughnut shoppe. I am. Little problems come up all the time and some of the people I work with stand there like deer in the headlights. Not me. I see a problem and I go to work solving it. That's what I like to do.

◙ **To me, problem-solving is kind of like a game** of 20 Questions. You try to get to the solution by asking the questions. What do you want to have happen here? How will you know when the problem is solved? What do you think the solution might look like? What are you trying to achieve? What are you trying to avoid? What do you want to get rid of? What do you want to hold onto? It's pretty fun going about problem-solving this way. Kind of like a game of Clue™. And when you think about it, Clue™ is all about deductive and inductive reasoning.

◙ **It's not like you have to be an expert** to be a problem-solver. In fact, there are too many experts these days. It's like there's an expert for everything. I think we all need to become more of the experts ourselves. Since when did going to an expert to solve a problem become better than solving it yourself?

◨ **When it comes to problem-solving**, the best piece of advice I ever heard was to keep the blinders off. Too many of us plow straight ahead in life without seeing as much as we should be seeing. Don't be so linear. You've got to look all around you, above you, below you. You never know where a good solution is going to come from.

◨ **A lot of my teachers** push brainstorming. In our physics class, we always worked in groups and it was brainstorming all the way. Somebody would bring in pizza and we'd sit around until we came up with some good ideas and possible solutions.

## The Creativity Factor

Many of us, when we think of creativity, immediately flash to people who were great writers or painters, but creativity does not belong solely to geniuses. We can all access creativity and develop it if we go about it the right way.

What exactly is creativity? Some people define it as the ability to take existing objects and put them together in different ways so that they can serve a new purpose. Somebody, for instance, thought of putting cotton on the end of a stick and coming up with the disposable swab. Let's have a look at how your fellow students view the issue of creativity.

◨ **The best way I've found** to make creativity happen is through sharing ideas. I gravitate toward people who I think are genuinely creative and I use them. Sounds terrible, but I don't mean it to be. I just like the way their minds work. So we'll have coffee together, or we might go to a movie or a concert and talk about what we've seen or heard. Their ideas and input get my creative juices going.

◉ **My older sister** is a painter, and a really good one. Really good and really serious. When I ask her how she keeps herself creative, she tells me that the rule is to "surprise your mind." That might mean taking a different route to work some mornings or eating dessert first or having breakfast for dinner. Pancakes in the evening will make your whole day feel different, and when your day feels different, it's easier for creativity to put in an appearance.

◉ **I like to watch my little nephews.** They're four and seven. They're never afraid to try things. They look at a problem and they're not worried that their solution won't work. They just go ahead and let it rip. Picasso said that every child is an artist, and I think he was right. The problem is how to remain an artist after you're all grown up.

◉ **You've got to work at your creativity.** You've got to understand that it takes more energy to be creative than not to be, but it's also more energizing. Sitting around watching TV is not going to energize you, you know that. But throwing a pot or knitting a sweater or having some fun with watercolors can be incredibly energizing.

◉ **Ever since I was in junior high**, I've kept a journal. I put down all kinds of ideas, crazy as they may be, without feeling the need to censor myself. I write in it every night, before I go to bed, just for a few minutes. That's enough for me to stay in touch with that inner part of me that if I'm not careful, can get lost in the daily routine.

◙ **Do you know about mind-mapping?** It's a really good way to access creative thinking, particularly if you're a visual person. If you're having a problem—let's say you're afraid to learn how to drive—you draw a picture of driving in the center. All around it you write words and phrases that come to mind when you think of driving like fast, accidents, honking horns, whatever. Use highlighter pens or symbols like stars or checks to emphasize the phrases that hit home the most. Study your mind-map and maybe some kind of pattern will emerge that will give you some insight into your problem.

---

### Learning Disabilities

While we're on the subject of how the brain works, we should spend a few moments talking about ways in which the brain is challenged. The cluster of disorders that affect people's ability to either interpret what they hear or to connect information from different parts of the brain is called learning disorders.

Learning disorders manifest themselves in a variety of ways. They can show themselves as specific difficulties with spoken or written language, or as problems with coordination, self-control, and/or the ability to pay attention. Learning disorders are generally classified within three groups: developmental speech and language disorders, academic skills disorders, and motor skills disorders.

One type of learning disorder that is particularly prevalent is Attention Deficit Disorder (ADD). It is closely connected to Attention Deficit/Hyperactivity Disorder (ADHD). These disorders are characterized by inattention, hyperactivity, and impulsivity, and they can be extremely counterproductive to scholastic achievement.

If you suspect that you may be suffering from a learning disorder—and many such disorders go undiagnosed and undocumented until late in life— talk to your teacher, your school guidance counselor, or the school psychologist. Testing may be warranted to determine if, in fact, you are in such a situation. You may also want to do some research into learning disorders in the library or on the Internet. A good Web site with which to begin is http://www.ldonline.org.

Now that we've looked at ways that the brain works, let's turn next to the issue of how we can develop good habits so that the work of the brain is made easier.

## Chapter 5

# STUDY SKILLS

In the preceding chapter, we offered a brief survey of how the brain works, the various types of intelligence, the mechanics of memory, and powerful ways to think. In this chapter, we'd like to focus in on the skills required to be a successful student.

Learning to be a good student is no different than learning to be a good driver or a good golfer or a good cook. You practice a set of positive habits—don't tailgate, don't slice to the right, don't oversalt—and the more you practice, the better you become. In this chapter, we will be looking at good study habits and hearing from your fellow students about what works for them.

# A Quiet Place to Study?

As a student, you'll need to find a quiet place to study where you won't be disturbed, right? A library is perfect or, failing that, maybe a padded cell?

Don't believe it. While the library could be the ideal study spot for many students, there is no such thing as a "right" or "wrong" place to study. Different study environments suit different people based on the different learning styles that characterize us.

A learning style can be defined as the way in which a person is most comfortable learning. There are three basic categories of learners: visual learners prefer to see whatever it is that they have to learn; auditory learners must listen in order to learn; and tactile/kinesthetic learners wish to touch or hold materials that are connected to the subject content they are studying. Let's look at how some of your fellow students identify themselves.

## Visual Learners

Visual learners like to see what they are being asked to learn. They appreciate graphs, diagrams, charts, illustrations, models, slides, videos, and such.

**When I see pages of text** without any illustrations, I go blank. The first things I always look at in a book are the illustrations. Now maybe that makes you think I should be sticking to comics or whatever, but I don't care. I know what I like, and I know I'm just as smart as anyone else.

▣ **I had this really traumatic year** back in fifth grade. I was given a seat in the back of the room, and I didn't know it at the time but I needed glasses. I saw very little of what was going on, and as a visual learner, I felt totally lost. From that point on, I made up my mind to always sit as close to the front as possible. Some of my friends make out like I'm a teacher's pet or something, but that's not it at all. I just need to see what's going on.

▣ **Being a visual learner**, I've found that color makes a huge difference for me. I have this whole system of using color markers to highlight my readings and notes and stuff. Pink is for super-important material, yellow is very important, green is if I have the time, and so on. My notes may look like the rainbow, but hey, rainbows are nice.

▣ **My mom** works in an ad agency, and knowing what a visual learner I am, she taught me this technique they use called storyboarding. It's basically telling a story in pictures, almost like a comic strip. So if I have a presentation I have to do in class, let's say, I'll draw myself going through the steps. It's a little weird maybe, but it helps me a lot.

▣ **Flashcards** are what saves my life. No matter what I'm studying, I'll always make up a set of flashcards for a test or whatever. It makes all the difference.

## Auditory Learners

These learners like to hear what they are being taught. They appreciate lectures, tapes, or anything they can listen to.

▣ **Being given a bunch of handouts** doesn't do it for me. I need to hear voices. I find that classroom discussion is what really reinforces the learning for me.

▣ **You know how they sell those tapes** "Learn Italian in the Car" or "Learn French in the Car? " To me, that's a really great way to learn something, so I figured, "Why not make my own tapes?" Now I take a tape recorder into class and tape my instructor's lectures, then I listen to them in the car to and from school or while I'm jogging, as many times as it takes for the material to sink in.

▣ **As long as I can hear something**, I'll remember it better. That means I can't work in a quiet place like a library because the way I study is to read my textbook out loud. The louder, the better. I even do it in the subway. I'll sit there reading my history textbook out loud, muttering all this stuff, and people give me this funny look, like I'm some crazed person who likes to talk to himself.

▣ **You know the expression**, "Say it with music?" Well, that's what I do. I sing what I have to learn. I take the information I have to memorize and I'll set it to some familiar song like the national anthem or whatever. It's kind of weird, but it doesn't hurt anyone and it works.

## Tactile/Kinesthetic Learners

These are the students who learn by moving, doing, and touching. They're the ones who go right to the "Touch-Me" part of the museum on the field trip.

▣ **A lot of tactile learners** like myself were labeled ADD—Attention Deficit Disorder—when we were younger. In my case, it took me a long time to shake off that label, which I never deserved in the first place. There was nothing wrong with me. I just had a learning style that my teachers didn't understand. Tactile learners like me learn best when we're allowed to move. If we can't move—if, in fact, we're punished for the way we are and are made to sit in our chairs—then it can become very difficult for us to learn.

▣ **If there's one thing** I've come to know about myself, it's that I need to take a lot of breaks when I'm studying. I need to stand up and walk around and go to the refrigerator and go to the bathroom and stretch and throw a ball to the dog. That's the way I learn. I'm a perfectly good tactile learner, so if anyone has a problem with that, it's their problem, not mine.

▣ **A lot of tactile learners** like myself also happen to be athletes. We've got that Body Smart intelligence. Knowing this about myself, I make accommodations to my learning style. Like I might study for a test while I'm on the treadmill. I've got a book rest rigged up and I can read just fine while I'm walking (running is a little harder).

◙ **I find that as a tactile learner**, I look for ways to satisfy my need to move while I'm studying. Any kind of movement helps, so one thing that I've learned to do is to hold something in my hand that I can move around and manipulate. A piece of clay, a smooth rock, any little thing like that goes a long way toward satisfying my needs. Even chewing gum helps.

◙ **Sometimes, I'll study** in a café or a bookstore that has a café in it because the feeling of movement around me—people coming and going and all that—is almost as good as my moving around myself.

# Setting Up a Study Space

In the best of all possible worlds, your study space will be in synch with your learning style. Some like it quiet, some like it lively. Whatever the mood (or the volume), you'll want to pay attention to other factors as well. Let's see what some of the students we interviewed had to say on this subject.

◙ **I need a door.** I can live without absolute quiet, but I'm easily distracted so doors are essential. A carrel in the library works pretty well for me, too. At least it's closed off on three sides.

◙ **No matter how small** or basically crummy your space is—I've got a wall in our downstairs rec room—you should still try to customize it with something that means something special to you and that makes the space more agreeable. I've got a bonsai tree on my desk, for instance. I'm just fascinated by it and every time I look at it, it's like a relief from my work. For somebody else, it could be an interesting paperweight or one of those babbling desk fountains you see around. A great screensaver is another approach.

◉ **My dad works at home**—he's a software designer—and he's like Mr. Efficient. You should see his office. He's got all these systems set up so that it feels like you're on a ship or something. Dad helped me set up systems of my own. I have everything in place—calculators, pencils, pencil sharpeners, file folders, magazine files, a dictionary—so I'm not always running out to get stuff at the store.

◉ **If you're really sensitive to noise** and don't have a private, quiet space to work in, check out earplugs. There are different kinds on the market now, and you're bound to find something that works for you.

◉ **No matter how great** your office is set up, if you're getting interruptions all the time, you're not going to get much work done. So, for me, one of the absolute necessities is to have an answering machine. I put it on and I don't even listen to hear who's calling until I'm finished with what I have to do.

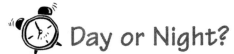 # Day or Night?

Once you've identified your learning style and have carved out a good place to study, the next step is to figure out the best time for you to get your work done. To determine this, it helps to have a sense of your biological clock.

What exactly is a biological clock? Think of it as a small group of brain cells that send and receive signals to and from other parts of the brain and the glands. A person's biological clock is not present at birth; newborns have no sense of a daily rhythm. During the first year of life, however, the biological clock kicks in, and as the years go by, it becomes increasingly sensitive to certain factors, chief among them daylight. Some people have biological clocks that are so sensitive to light that when the light is diminished, as in autumn and winter, they may become sleepy or depressed, and may even need light therapy. (See more about this in Chapter 8, Holistic Hints). Although some people classify themselves as night owls and others as early birds, research shows that most people do not function as well at night as during the day. In any case, disturbed daily rhythms caused by poor sleep can upset a person's metabolism and appetite, and can result in headaches and overeating in an attempt to comfort oneself. It is important, therefore, to understand your biological clock and to work with it.

▣ **My mother's always on me** because I'm not bright and cheery in the morning. I can't help it. I'm a night person. Given the choice, I'd always prefer staying up late to getting up early.

◙ **I would say, by nature**, that I'm a morning person, but I've got to stay up late at night or I just won't get everything done that I need to get done. So I guess I'm working against my biological clock, and maybe that's a terrible thing, but it's what I have to do at this stage of my life.

◙ **I'm not actually that sensitive** to whether it's day or night. I'm kind of a compulsive person, so if I have work to do, I just do it. I can block out almost anything and I can work almost anywhere, anytime. I'll always carry my work with me wherever I go. If I go to the dentist or I'm waiting for a bus or whatever, I'll use that time to study. Hey, it's not like I've got anything better to do, and that way I don't use up my minutes talking on my cell phone.

◙ **To me, it's not the issue of night or day** as much as it is the issue of routines. I think it's really important to establish routines whenever and wherever you can in your life. I know that every day at five I exercise. Every morning when I wake up, I throw in my laundry while I'm getting ready for the day; I study without any distractions between nine and eleven in the evening. I know what to expect and when. Sure, things come up now and then to throw me off my routines, but having the routines in the first place grounds me enough so that I can get back to them soon, without having lost a lot of momentum.

**On the advice of my grandmother**, I made a great discovery: naps! Naps are amazing. They totally refuel me. A 10-minute nap, or even a five-minute one, can keep me going for hours. Try it.

# Approaching Your Textbook

Okay, now that we've had a look at the environmental issues around studying—when to do it and where to do it—let's get down to the nitty-gritty. Textbooks are a good place to start. Almost every course you take will have a textbook, and textbooks are written in their own special way. At first, a textbook may look like a great big monster—1,000 pages on economics, let's say, or psychology—but good textbooks are written to be user-friendly. You just have to know how to use them. One technique to keep in mind is called previewing. To preview a book means to scan the part you're assigned to read. You look for main points and organization. It's sort of like getting the big picture before you focus in on the elements that make up the big picture.

**The first thing I do** when I start a chapter is to look at all the headings and other organizational clues. Just about everything you have to know that's important is flagged. It's either going to be in bold type or italics, or there are bullets next to them (the little round black dots that are easy for your eye to pick out).

◙ **The thing I like** about most of the textbooks that are being put out today is that they take the visual learner into account. My mom has some of her old textbooks from college and they look so dry and stuffy. Ours are full of pictures—a lot of them in color—and cool graphs and stuff.

◙ **I always go** to the end of the chapter first, to the review section, to get a good idea of what's really the most important stuff in the chapter. Then, when I've got that overview, I'll go back and start reading because the plan of the chapter is in my head.

◙ **I mark up my book** a lot when I read. I use highlighters and put stars next to important stuff. Let's just say I customize it.

◙ **There's a myth** that you've got to read every word of a textbook assignment. Not so. There are often little "extras," sidebar columns, for instance, that have information that may be interesting but that isn't crucial. The main ideas make themselves known. They're usually right out there, in big bold letters, where they can't be missed.

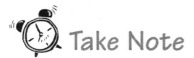 Take Note

By now, it is quite evident that if you hope to succeed as a student, you'll have to master the fine art of note-taking. The ideas and information that your instructor delivers in the course of his presentation are far too complex for you to try to keep all in your head. It simply won't work. The good news is that note-taking is a skill that can be learned, like every other skill we've talked about so far. Here are some pointers that your fellow students would like to share with you.

## Overview

Here are some general pointers to keep in mind in any situation where you're taking notes.

◉ **If I know** I'm going to be in a lecture or some other situation where I'm going to have to take notes, I'll sit right up front. That way, all possible distractions are literally behind me.

◉ **Taking notes is a job**, and like every other job, you've got to come prepared. You'll need a couple of pens (one might run dry) and paper and some bottled water so you don't have to get up for a drink if you're thirsty.

◉ **When someone's giving a lecture** or a talk or some kind of presentation, the expectation is that they'll structure it with a beginning or introduction, a middle, and an end or summary, so it's easy to follow. The introduction and summary are particularly important. The introduction lets you know where you're going. It orients you for the whole thing, so make sure you don't miss it. Don't come in late to a lecture. Bad idea.

◉ **If the instructor is any good**, he's going to cue you as he goes along. He'll say things like, "First" or "Next" or "For example." You've got to learn to pick up on those cues. Some instructors will even cue you really directly, saying things like, "This is important. You've got to know this" or even, "This is going to be on the test." Those are the instructors I like best.

◉ **The point of taking notes** is not to get every word down. That's impossible. Put the instructor's words into your words. You want to understand what she says, not duplicate what she says.

## Specific Strategies

Here are some things you can start doing right now to make sure that your note-taking is as effective as possible.

◉ **Whenever the instructor** emphasizes something, I'll put a big star next to that point with my highlighter. You know that's going to be on the test.

◉ **Do you know about abbreviating?** Like, instead of writing "and," you can make a plus sign (+). Or, if it allows you to write faster, you can leave out letters of recognizable words, like writing Cnstitutn for instance, instead of writing out Constitution. You save a lot of note-taking time with those little tricks.

◉ **A really good strategy** for note-taking is to use the two-column format. You make one column wide and one narrow. In the narrow one, you jot down the important thoughts you pick out as you review all the main ideas and important facts in the wide column.

◙ **It's generally a good idea** to use an outline form when you take notes. You don't have to make it literally an outline, with Roman numerals and A, B, and C and all that. But you should at least use indentations so that you can see, at a glance, the relationship of the main ideas to the supporting points.

◙ **I always try to go over my notes** right after the presentation to make sure that I got it all down and that I can understand what I wrote. It's a good idea to do that while the material is still fresh in your mind.

# Getting to Know Your Library

Now that you're becoming a serious student, you have to develop a comfortable relationship with the library because you're going to be spending a lot of time there. Maybe your idea of a library is that it's a place where stern people shush you all the time amid row after row of dusty books. If that's the case, then you're way out of touch with the times. The library today is fully reflective of all the astounding technology that is changing our lives, and it is a place that you will find fascinating if you give it half a chance.

◙ **Start with the librarian.** The librarian is there to help you. That's part of the job description. If a particular librarian is not helpful, ask to speak with another librarian until you find one who is. Generally, librarians are eager to help you learn how to access the power of the library. They get off on it, and why shouldn't they? The library is a pretty powerful, awesome place.

▣ **If you think a library** is mostly about books, think again. It's about books, periodicals (that's magazines and journals, in library-speak), reference works, online materials, CD-ROMs, and so much more.

▣ **Finding periodicals** is a whole other matter. Generally, you use different periodical indexes to find what you need. Asking your librarian is the best shortcut.

▣ **You don't even have to leave home** these days to be a great researcher. I mean, it's good to go to the library and all, but a lot of my research is done on-line, on my laptop, right from my bed (which is where I like to work). I can get into Web sites of companies, organizations, government agencies, all kinds of data bases, libraries around the world, discussion groups, and list serves on various topics. It's amazing.

# Internet Research

The Internet is an amazing thing, but you have to know how to use it. Here are some important tips to keep in mind to make the most of your on-line experience.

▣ **Focus your search.** Don't just go to the net to start your thinking because if you're not focused, you can get distracted by a zillion different sites. In fact, it's a good idea to actually write down what you're looking for. The ten most intelligent animal species. The five main reasons for the outbreak of the Civil War. That kind of thing.

▣ **Pick a good search engine** and start out with the one you like best. Some people are loyal to http://www.google.com now because it's new and super-fast. Others like old standbys like http://www.yahoo.com or http://www.altavista.com. New ones come out all the time, so ask around and see what people are using and liking.

▣ **Keywords are all important** for narrowing your search. For instance, if your keyword is World War II, then you'll get seven million entries coming up. If it's The Battle of the Bulge, you'll get a lot less. If it's "Casualties in the Battle of the Bulge," you'll get even less. If you want only sites called up that have to do with the thing you're looking for, then put quotes around your keywords. "Battle of the Bulge" instead of battle bulge will keep a lot of weight-reducing sites from popping up.

▣ **I think the greatest thing** about the Internet is that it frees you up to e-mail just about anyone. If you find an article about quasars by some professor at a specific university and you want to ask him a question, just get his e-mail from the university Web site and e-mail him the question. Nine times out of ten, I find that authorities will e-mail you back.

🔲 **One of the biggest issues** with Internet research is the reliability of the information you get. There is a lot of junk out there. Some ways of determining if your information is for real is by asking some key questions. Does the site claim to be the official Web site of a company or organization that you've actually heard something about? Can you find a physical address anywhere on the site? If the site claims to be connected to a government agency or office, does it have "gov" in the Web address? And when you cite the site, give the complete URL, not just the address of the home page.

In this chapter, we've had a look at the general study skills you'll need to make it as a student. Let's go to a more specific skill in the next chapter—test-taking—and see how to handle that high-stress event, along with all the other stress in your life.

## Chapter 6

# TESTING AND OTHER HIGH STRESS EVENTS

**S**ome people are afraid of spiders, some people fear heights, and some people can't handle the idea of flying. Being in the grip of such fears may create difficulties in a person's life, but to a large extent and with some careful arranging, these scary things can more or less be avoided. A person can stay away from the woods where spiders lurk, take trains instead of planes, and keep away from hot air balloons and rooftop revolving restaurants. But one of the most common fears—the fear of taking tests—is not only one of the most difficult to avoid but also can have a huge impact on a person's life. Test anxiety is so powerful in certain individuals that it can make those afflicted feel physically ill. If left untreated, test anxiety can mushroom into a full-blown phobia that can undermine an otherwise rewarding school experience. In this chapter, we will first discuss how you can overcome test anxiety, and we will then move on to the issue of handling stress in general.

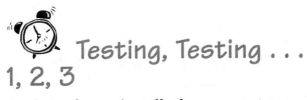

# Testing, Testing . . . 1, 2, 3

For those of you who suffer from test anxiety, you know the telltale signs: sweaty palms, clammy pallor, unsettled stomach. Not a pretty picture, is it? Test anxiety can definitely affect how you perform on an exam and can impact on how you do in school, but the good news is that this fear *can* be overcome. All you need is a little insight and some behavior modification to deal with even the most severe cases of test anxiety.

## Before You Even Start

There are things you can do before you even arrive at the test center to help prevent some of the anxiety.

◉ **What's the best antidote** to test anxiety? Knowing that you're well prepared. If you can honestly say that you've done what you were supposed to do to get ready for this exam, you may not even feel that nervous. But you've got to be honest. Ask yourself: Did you go to all your classes? Did you keep up with the work? A lot of times, the anxiety gets overwhelming because it's fed by the guilt that comes with having procrastinated and not doing what you know you should have done.

◉ **If you've got an exam scheduled**, check in with your instructor ahead of time to see if maybe you can take a practice exam. A lot of instructors will allow that and it's a great way to build up confidence.

◉ **For me**, taking a test is like running a 5K race. I've got to prepare myself mentally and physically. That means the night before—and for sure in the morning—I don't drink a lot of coffee or cola or eat junk food. Instead, I try to calm myself with some good carbs like brown rice or fruits and vegetables. Maybe I'll listen to some Mozart or Celtic music, something to relax me. And, most of all, I'll try to get a good night's sleep. That's so important.

◉ **Whatever you do**, make sure you give yourself plenty of time to get to your test. The worst thing is to come rushing in, all out of breath, having stressed yourself out looking for a parking spot or whatever. Adding stress to stress is like adding fat to fire.

◉ **I'm a social person**, but when it comes to tests, I resist my impulses. I always sit by myself when I take an exam. What I really don't need is to pick up on somebody else's anxiety. Anxiety is contagious. Avoid it like the plague!

## Taking Control

Just about everyone suffers from some degree of test anxiety. For some people, it's butterflies in the stomach.

For others, it's seagulls. Getting a grip on the anxiety before it gets its grip on you is the key.

🔲 **Tests are a drag**—there's no two ways around it—but I've finally figured out how to handle them. First of all, I tell myself, "It's only a test." Even if it's a huge test, what's the worst that's going to happen if I fail? I'll have to take it again? I'll have to do better the next time? Okay, so that's not the end of the world. You have to remember that everyone fails at something at some time or another. If you fail, it doesn't mean you're bad. It just means you're human.

🔲 **Okay, people.** Just because you've got a little test anxiety is no reason to freak out. Everybody gets it and you know what? It's not the worst thing in the world. In fact, it can really help if you think about the anxiety as having a constructive aspect to it. A little anxiety can actually get you up for the thing you have to do. I'm an actor, and when I go out on stage on opening night, I've got butterflies in my stomach. But I don't go crazy from it. I realize that the anxiety is there to get me focused, to get that adrenaline pumping so that I can do what I have to do. That's what it's like with test anxiety, for me, anyway. It boosts me up onto another plateau of focus and as long as I can keep it in bounds, it's actually good for me.

🔲 **If ever there was a time** for positive self-talk, it's when you're about to take a test. That's the time to be good to yourself. A lot of people choose that time to let all kinds of negative internal voices come out, voices that say things like, "You always screw up on tests" or "You're the dumbest one in the room" or "If you mess up on this one, it's over." Your job is to control those negative thoughts with the Stop Thought approach. When you feel those kinds of thoughts coming on, you have to literally say to yourself, "Stop Thought." It's like holding up a sign. And then you replace those negative thoughts with positive ones, telling yourself things like, "You've really prepared yourself well for this one" or "You did well on the last test, so there's no reason why you shouldn't do okay on this one." Be your own best friend and see what happens.

◙ **The worst mistake you can make** when you're taking a test is to start looking around the room to see how everyone else is doing. "Oh, look at Kevin. He's already packing up." Just mind your own business. That way, you won't distract yourself.

◙ **There've been a few times** when I've been in a test situation and I've gotten totally overwhelmed by anxiety. What I learned to do at times like that is to just turn over the test, close my eyes, take three or four deep breaths, and ride out the feeling. It'll usually passes.

## Test-Taking Strategies
Here are a few choice ways to think about "beating the system" when it comes to test-taking.

◙ **My test strategy begins like this:** Do the easiest questions first. Getting those under your belt will give you the confidence to go on to the harder ones.

▣ **Here's how I always begin** a test: I do a first pass, giving it a quick once-over, and I mark any questions I don't know right off with the idea that I'll go back to them later. I don't want to waste time getting stuck on any one question.

▣ **Keep an eye out** for any clues that are in the make-up of the questions themselves. For instance, if you're doing a True or False section, the words *always* or *never* can often indicate a false statement.

## It's Almost Over . . .

You can see the light at the end of the tunnel. But that doesn't necessarily mean you're home free as far as the anxiety goes.

▣ **Whatever you do**, don't panic when other students start to hand in their papers. Sometimes, they'll do that because they're giving up, not because they know the stuff better than you do.

▣ **When I finish a test**, I absolutely refuse to go over it with my friends. It drives them crazy but I'm sorry; it just makes me more anxious. Instead, I reward myself. I'll stop in at the bakery and buy myself something I wouldn't normally eat—a big fat devil's food cupcake, let's say—and I'll tell myself that at least it's over for now.

▣ **One thing that I've come to understand** is that if I don't understand a question, it may be because it's not a very well-written test. You know, a person can get an F on creating a test just like you can get an F taking one. If I think something on a test is wrong or vague or whatever, I'll ask the instructor about it. Quite a few times, I've won my point and my grade goes up.

---

## Instant Relaxation

When you find yourself feeling extremely nervous—freaking out even—try one of the following "instant relaxer" methods to help you get past the problem.

✱ *Guided imagery.* Imagine yourself in a place that you really love and that you find totally relaxing. Maybe it's a beach where you can watch the sea lions playing in the water. Maybe it's a baseball game on a warm summer night as you eat a hot dog or crackerjacks. Whatever it is, go to that place—in your mind—and let it comfort you.

✱ *Progressive relaxation.* Start at your toes and say, "Relax your toes." Work your way up your body, inch by inch: relax your knees, relax your belly, relax your chest, and so on. The higher up you go, the bigger the relaxation payoff. But keep in mind that this takes practice.

---

# Stress: A Societal Epidemic

Look around you at the people you know. What do you see? A lot of them are experiencing discomfort, aren't they? They're suffering from headaches, poor digestion, low energy, aches and pains. Some of them can't sleep at night. A lot of them are overeating, and some are undereating. And you don't even know about their overall lack of enjoyment in day-to-day life. So what's going on here?

The answer is stress. Too much of it. And it's happening on every level of our society and throughout the world. So much so that the World Health Organization has designated it as an epidemic.

What is stress? It can be defined as an environmental condition that causes physiologic changes (those that have to do with our bodies), cognitive changes (those that alter the way we think), emotional changes, and behavioral changes. For instance, let's imagine that you are about to take a final exam in some subject that has not exactly been a picnic for you, physics, for instance. As you sit down and get out your pencils and your bottled water and your mints, you begin to realize that you are in an environment that is causing you distress, big-time. The physiological changes are there: your palms are sweaty, your hands are cold, your heart is pounding, and your head aches. Emotional changes also may be present: you could be feeling panic, despair, or who knows what. Behavioral changes? Maybe you're giddy, and much to the annoyance of those around you, you are chattering your head off. Cognitive changes? You bet. You're so stressed out you can't tell the difference between quantum and quasar.

In other words, you're in big trouble.

Stress is a nasty, counterproductive, self-defeating thing. Too much of it can be a killer. Stress can impact in very serious ways on your body and is a huge health concern. The question is why are we feeling it so much?

There are a lot of answers to that big question. To start out with, many of us are seriously sleep-deprived, thanks to the necessity of working more than one job and also, in large part, because of the temptations of television, video, the Internet, and other such electronic distractions. What' s more, Americans don't get nearly enough vacation time. Issues like child care and health insurance can become sources of major stress for our citizens. All of that stress is made worse when we, as commuters, find ourselves on congested thoroughfares trying to get to our jobs or school on time. And all of the above is routine, everyday stress, which doesn't take into account the major stressors that occur in people's lives like the death of a loved one, illness, accidents, divorce, job layoffs, and so on. So how are you supposed to deal with that kind of stress? Let's have a look.

▣ **Half the time**, I might not even know how stressed I am until somebody points it out to me. "You're not eating" or "Look how fast you're eating" or "Why are you grinding your teeth that way?" Then I'll stop and think about what I'm doing, and sure enough, I'm like totally stressed out. I'll see myself in the mirror and I'll say, "Whoa. Who *is* that person?"

▣ **When I'm stressed**, all I want to do is sleep. It's like I'm dragging myself around. I go home, I eat cereal for dinner, I go to sleep, I make myself wake up. Sometimes, I'm worried that the day will come when I won't make myself get out of bed. That's called a nervous breakdown, isn't it?

▣ **I hate to even tell you** what I do when I get stressed out. I eat. And eat. And eat. I'm talking tons of chocolate and caramel corn and, well, everything I can get my hands on. Then I get into this diet–binge cycle and that makes me even more stressed.

▣ **Hey, it's not the end of the world** to have some stress in your life. These days, the media tell us that if we have stress we're going to keel over. Do you really think that there's ever been a time in history when people didn't feel stress? Like, when they were burning people at the stake or marching off to the Crusades or when the Black Death was hitting London. You think that was any bed of roses?

▣ **I always thought** I was basically okay at handling stress, and then this year happened. Everything's gone wrong. I was in a car accident and broke my leg. My boyfriend and I split up. My mom got a virus that turned into endocarditis and she had to spend two weeks in the hospital. I tried handling the stress with meditation and exercise and all that, but it wasn't working so I got on an anti-anxiety drug. I'm not going to be on it forever, but for now, it's really helped me get through the bad stuff.

## Recognizing Signs of Stress

Stress impacts us in a wide variety of ways.

* *Physical.* Digestive problems, headache, neck pain, skin rashes, muscle tension, elevated blood pressure, flare-ups of illnesses like arthritis or asthma

* *Thought processes.* Memory issues, impatience, procrastination, obsessive behavior.

* *Emotional.* Depression, irritability, helplessness, anxiety, anger, bitterness, conflicts with coworkers.

If you are suffering from these sorts of symptoms, consult with your physician to determine the best course of action.

# Stress Relief

There are two basic routes to stress relief: changing or modifying your behavior and finding and using whatever methods help you to control the stress you're experiencing. Let's start by looking at the behavior modification that may be necessary.

## Assertiveness

Ask yourself, Are you the kind of person who always feels that you're being forced into doing something you don't want to do? Do you have a hard time expressing your feelings and saying no? If so, you are probably feeling put upon a great deal of the time and this may be causing you stress. Fortunately, there are proven methods that can help you become a more assertive person who feels more in control of things.

What exactly is assertiveness? Let's think of it as the ability to express yourself and your rights without violating the rights of other individuals. Assertiveness is the opposite of road rage, wherein your expression takes a completely aggressive and destructive form. An assertive person expresses thoughts and feelings in a way that clearly states his or her underlying needs. A person who is able to become positively assertive is also able to keep open the lines of communication with others.

To become assertive—and, again, we want you to think of this as a positive word—you should have a firm understanding of your rights as a human being. The Constitution is founded on the belief that all Americans have the rights of life, liberty, and the pursuit of happiness. Your personal "Constitution" should include those same three, of course, but you should also understand that you have the right to decide on how to live your life. Your goals and dreams should be your own. You have the right to claim your own values, beliefs, and opinions. You have the right to express yourself. That means saying "No" or "I don't understand" or whatever else you wish to say. You have the right to ask for information and help as you need it. You have the right to make mistakes and to fail at something, as long as you understand that you are the one who will be dealing with the after-effects of your decisions.

Assertiveness is different—very different—from selfishness. Selfishness rides roughshod over the rights of other people. Assertiveness expresses a person's own rights with the understanding that individuals must co-exist. Assertiveness is no magic bullet. It will not cure you of all your problems but it will allow you to say "no" or "yes" as the situation arises. And for many people, learning how to say "no" or "yes" is half the battle.

Let's look at some ways that your fellow students have learned how to make assertiveness a part of their lives.

▣ **I've learned** to live by two small words: Be clear. Let people know what's on your mind and let them know in a way that is to the point and on target.

▣ **I practice using certain key phrases** like *I want to* or *I don't want to. I disagree* is another one. These are the kinds of expressions by which you can make yourself clear without any display of anger.

▣ **Assertiveness** comes more easily and more effectively when you have one-on-one exchanges with people. If you have a problem with something that someone has done, don't tell the person through someone else or when you're in a group situation with that person. Take it into a private corner somewhere.

▣ **One of the rules** of assertiveness is to own the feeling you're having. That means if you have a problem with something, put it in personal terms. "I don't agree with what you said," is a far better thing to say to somebody than "you're wrong," which leaves no room to go anywhere.

◉ **Part of getting good** at assertiveness has to do with allowing for feedback. Keep in mind that assertiveness doesn't mean it's all about you. The point of assertiveness is to keep the lines of communication open. Saying things like "Am I making myself clear?" or "What are your feelings about this?" are ways to be assertive and yet still make it clear that you're looking for a dialogue.

---

### Learning to Say "No"

Learning to say "no" is the hardest thing in the world for some people. You've got to practice it, because if you don't get it down, you'll find yourself chronically overloaded, often to the point of desperation. Practicing in front of a mirror can be a helpful way to overcome your problem with the N word. Role-play this exchange between two siblings for instance:

*Jack:*   Hey, Tina. Can I use your car on Saturday?

*Tina:*   Why?

*Jack:*   I want to go watch Paul's game. It's the sectionals.

*Tina:*   I need it for errands.

*Jack:*   Come on. Just this once.

---

*Tina:* That's what you said last time.

*Jack:* Oh, give me a break.

*Tina:* I'd like to help you, Jack. Maybe I can drive you where you need to go. But I need the car. I'm sorry, but the answer is no.

Saying "no" wasn't easy for Tina and it may not be easy for you. It may take a lot of practice. But don't give up. You can do it!

# Stress Do's and Don'ts

Now that we've looked at some of the "big picture" issues around stress, let's focus in on some of the many ways that you can control and relieve your stress so that it won't get the best of you. Remember that in this modern world of ours, you're never going to be completely stress-free. To achieve that goal, you might have to become a Buddhist monk living in a monastery in the Himalayas somewhere, although, these days, there really is no immunity from stress wherever you are. But these tips from your fellow students will certainly help you balance the scale when it feels like it's going to tilt. Let's start with what *not* to do.

## Stress Don'ts

◉ **Don't eat junk food.** The stuff that people shovel into their mouths when they're stressed—colas, fried foods, chips, white sugar—just puts more stress on their bodies. When I know I'm going to be in a high-stress situation, I make sure that I get my B vitamins and calcium. Eating a lot of raw foods will also help me get through a stress situation.

◉ **When I'm stressed**, I steer clear of caffeine. Taking in a lot of caffeine when I'm stressed is like throwing fat on the fire. I reach for the chamomile instead. And, of course, don't smoke, ever!

◉ **You know what's a fast way** to eliminate half the stress in your life? Ending unhealthy relationships, if that's what you're into. I know it's not that easy, but it's got to be done, and you might as well bite the bullet and do it. Unhealthy relationships are the number one leading cause of stress. They're toxic!

◉ **A good way to reduce stress** in your life is to reduce the noise level in your life. Turn off the hip-hop. Turn off the TV. The world is a stressful place. You turn on the news and you hear all about war and people dying and the economy going belly up. If you can't handle that kind of stress, then steer clear of it. Does that mean you're an ostrich putting your head in the sand? Well, if you are, and if that's what you need to do to survive, at least for a while, then so be it. Enjoy the quiet or try listening to some calming music for a change.

◻ **Don't go on buying sprees** to make yourself feel better. Live within your means. If you're spending more than you're making and running up crazy credit card bills, you're going to feel stress. Boy, are you going to feel stress. Is that extra sweater or pair of shoes really worth it?

## Stress Do's

There are many methods that people can choose from to reduce their stress levels. Experiment to see what works for you.

◻ **The best stress relief**—better than anything—is deep breathing. It calms you and energizes you at the same time. You can do it anywhere, anytime. It doesn't cost anything. It can lower blood pressure. Now you're going to ask me how you can breathe deeply when you're feeling stressed and can't get a deep breath, right? Good question. It's something you learn how to do. Go take a yoga class and find out. I also like to do deep breathing with a twist. When I'm stressed, I tell myself to "breathe in the good" as I'm breathing in and "breathe out the bad" as I'm breathing out. You'd be amazed what a great stress-buster this can be.

◻ **My cure for stress** is sleep. I know a lot of people can't sleep when they're stressed, but for me, it's the opposite. I get into bed before 10 P.M. with some Celtic music on and I'm good for eight hours.

◻ **You want to know how** I beat stress? By giving myself goodies. Whenever I've come through a rough patch where I've been running myself ragged, I reward myself with a special treat. Maybe it's a fruit smoothie, maybe it's an afternoon movie, maybe it's a nap. Or maybe it's a nap with a friend!

◙ **Laughing helps.** When I'm stressed out, I turn off the news on the car radio and I put on a comedy tape. When I laugh, I can feel the stress just fly out of me. Oddly enough, crying can help, too. I don't mean wallowing in self-pity. I mean putting on some great old movie where the heroine is going to die but doesn't tell her lover until it's over and you've got four handkerchiefs going and you can feel all that stress just oozing from your body in the form of tears.

◙ **For me, it's hobbies.** I like to go beachcombing. I could spend hours looking for beach glass in the sand. It transports me away from every care I have in the world.

As we've said, you shouldn't expect to completely eliminate stress from your life. In the terribly intense world in which we live, there is no such thing as a stress-free environment; not for you, not for anyone. The goal for most people in the 21st century is to manage the stress and to control it so it doesn't take you over. One easy and productive way to keep stress under control is to make sure that you're as organized and on top of things as possible. There is nothing as stressful as spending an hour looking for your keys or your eyeglasses when they were in the glove compartment of your car all along. Why put up with it?

Well, the good news, which you'll read all about in the next chapter, is that you don't have to put up with it. You can acquire a whole new set of habits that saves you time—and lots of stress—and that ups your productivity enormously.

## Chapter 7

# GETTING ORGANIZED

*Be prepared.*
*Neatness counts.*
*Dot your I's and cross your T's.*

T hese expressions, which you've probably
heard from parents, teachers, and other
authority figures all your life, may make you
crazy. They may be exactly the opposite of how you
think and how you like to view the world. Maybe
you see yourself as a free spirit, a square peg amid
round holes, a person who likes to do things your
own way. But no matter how free-spirited or talented
or artistic one may be, the fact is that we all need to
have a certain level of organizational skills to get
through the day. Perhaps your responsibilities as a
student are convincing you of that need. Maybe
you're even coming to realize that over the years,
you've consistently fallen short of that organized
ideal and you'd like to make up for lost time. If so,
we resoundingly reply, "Better late than never."

Since we've brought up the issue of your history as a student, let's look back to when you were a lot younger. Honestly now, were you that kid in third grade who was always forgetting your pencils, your notebook, and your lunch? Mrs. Smithers got pretty grumpy with you, didn't she? Chances are, there was a little boy or girl in your class who never forgot anything, who always had the pencils, the notebook, and the lunch. Mrs. Smithers loved that kid, didn't she? No doubt, that student went right to the head of the class. Well, it's not third grade anymore. A lot of time has passed and a lot of growing has gone on, and now you're ready and eager to be recognized for the good work that you do. You're talented and bright and interested in the world. You deserve recognition. So why handicap yourself? Isn't it time to stop forgetting things and to start remembering what's important? After all, when you move out of your schooling phase into the work world, you will be encountering a whole other set of expectations, and people will be far less forgiving of forgetfulness, lack of punctuality, and other such signs of poor organization. Now is the time in your life to develop those good habits that you will need to get ahead.

Being highly organized won't automatically send you to the head of the class but it certainly will help. Being disorganized means that you'll be wasting too much time and will probably have to repeat your tasks. Do you really have the time for that at this point in your life?

Getting organized and managing your time is part art, part science, and part pure determination. Even if it is not in your basic nature to be terribly organized, you can still make significant improvements in that department if you put your mind to doing so. In this chapter, you will be reading a lot of tips on the subject of organization. Some of what we'll be presenting is broad-based and general. Also included in this chapter will be a round-up of quick time-saving tips that you can use in many different areas of your life. Taken all together, the advice in this chapter should point your toward a much easier and more productive place.

 Time Management

There's no time like the present to start talking about time and what it means to you. So what does it mean to you?

## It's About Time

Time is a very sensitive issue. People who are chronically late wear out the patience of others. In fact, some people use their lateness as a passive form of aggression. As a student, now is the time to think about how you can best use your time. There are only so many hours in the day and chances are you're juggling school, work obligations, and family and social obligations. If you fail to make the most of your time, you run the risk of falling seriously behind, and the more you fall behind, the harder it gets to catch up.

▣ **Time is a big issue** in my family. My mom's always late for everything while my Dad always wants everyone to be early. It drives me crazy and I wish they'd just do their own thing and let me do mine. You know, I read somewhere that every person has an "inner organizer." It's like a natural clock you carry around inside yourself. Some people have a nice quiet clock that keeps good time; others have clocks that tick loud and fast and that don't always work. The point is to find out which clock you have and then listen to it.

▣ **I've always been known** for coming to class late. I just have a really hard time organizing myself. I leave stuff behind in one class and have to run back to get it, which makes me late for the next class. I think some of my teachers hate me for this.

▣ **I'm sorry**, I'm not going to walk around with a clipboard and a stopwatch like I'm timing heats at a meet. I don't want to live that way. If there are times when I'm late, then I'm late. If you ask me, the point is to create a system that speaks to the way you like to live. Some people get off on living by the clock; others need to be more flexible. I'm one of those "others." I could try to change, I suppose, but, deep down, I know I'll never be other than who I am. A mostly organized—but sometimes really disorganized—human being.

▣ **I think we live** in altogether too much of an overscheduled world. I really mean it. It's like everyone's running around with their organizers and their cell phones and heaven forbid you might be a little late getting somewhere! It's such a one-sided way of looking at life. I try to have a sense of what I need to do generally such as I need to get that big paper done by Monday or I need to buy my mother a Mother's Day gift. But even with these goals in mind, I still want to have some feeling of flexibility. If there's a solar eclipse, or even a rainbow, I want to be able to stop and look at it. If I'm sitting in a café with some person having an incredible, life-altering conversation, I don't want to have to jump up at 11:43 because the dog has to be walked. You know what I mean?

## Getting a Handle on It

Okay, so we agree that time is a complicated issue. How do we get started on making our peace with it? Here are some ideas from your fellow students.

◉ **If you think about it**, the issue of time management is very much linked to the issue of assertiveness. If you can't learn to say "no," then people are always going to be taking advantage of you and using up your time however they see fit.

◉ **If I really want to get things done**, I have to be direct with people almost to the point of rudeness. Someone might call me on my cell and say "Do you have a minute?" and I'm like "No." If I don't say "no," I know I'm just going to get myself into a whole lot of trouble.

◙ **Some people** can handle interruptions better than other people. I'm not good at it. Particularly if I'm trying to study. So I set down rules with my friends and my family: "Do not call me between the hours of 8 and 10." I don't care what's happening. I don't care if Cousin Melissa just announced her engagement or if Sarah met the man of her dreams or any of it. No one is allowed to call me unless it's a life or death situation.

◙ **I "give" people time.** I think of it as a little gift. If my mother suddenly wants to talk to me about this outfit she saw on sale at the department store, I say, "Okay, Ma, you've got five minutes." If my friend Angie calls me up and wants to ask me if I think she should color her hair red, I'll say, "Okay, Angie, you've got five minutes." Five minutes is as much of a gift as I want to give anyone when I've got so much pressure on me to get things done. And if people don't like it, that's just the way it's going to have to be for a while. Until I get over the hump—until I feel confident that I've got all my obligations under control—then I'm going to have to be pretty tight with the time.

 ## Making Lists

Okay, so maybe you don't think of yourself as a "list" sort of person. We respect your right to define who you are. But a word of advice: maybe you ought to rethink your position. Because the fact is, there are very busy people who can survive without them. Keeping a "to-do" list could be just the thing to move your days from chaos to control. Whether you use a memo pad, a pocket calendar, an electronic organizer, a stick-it pad, or a ballpoint pen on the palm of your hand, don't leave home without it! And once you start keeping a daily to-do list, you may also find that a weekly or even monthly to-do list has a lot to recommend it, too.

▣ **I've been keeping a to-do list** for a couple of years now and it's made a big difference in my life. I've gotten into the habit of starting my day off by reviewing my list. I'll sit down with a cup of coffee, and if it's a good day, a banana muffin, and I'll look it over really carefully. If I can do this in a relatively peaceful, calm moment, I feel like I've got half the battle won. I'm starting out with some kind of handle on the day and that's worth a lot.

▣ **There's one rule** I never break, and if you're smart, you might want to do the same: keep your to-do list to one side of one page. If you've got a to-do list that can't fit on one side of one page, that means you've got too much "to do!" Also, unless you're the kind of person who does crossword puzzles in pen, always write your to-do list in pencil because you know it's going to change. That's the nature of a to-do list: it's a work in progress. Things get canceled and shuffled around all the time.

▣ **Everybody** has their own way of keeping to-do lists. Mine has two columns. One column says

"HARD," the other says "EASY." I like to group things this way because that means I can schedule an easy block in the day and if I know I have that, I can get through the hard parts.

◉ **When I make up a to-do list**, I always try to keep in mind what kind of energy I can expect to have at different points in the day. I try not to schedule stuff that takes a lot of energy in the four o'clock slot, for instance, because that's when I'm usually dragging myself around. And I never put down more than 10 items on a list in one day. If I can manage to get 10 or nine or even eight solid things done, that's a good day. Seven is okay. Five or six is passable. Three or four means that something's wrong. Maybe I'm getting the flu or something. One or two means I've got the flu and I'm flat on my back in bed.

◉ **Everybody's got** their own method, but my "sanity secret" is to schedule in at least one block of free time a day. No matter how packed the day is that's coming up, I'll still factor in free time. That way, I've got protection in case something unexpected comes along, like car trouble or my dog running away or whatever. And something unexpected always does come up, doesn't it?

## Prioritization

The organizational principle of prioritization— attacking tasks in the order of their importance—is critical to the skill of making lists.

◉ **A to-do list** doesn't make sense unless you prioritize it. You need to put the most important thing at the top of your list. In other words, Biology Final or Late Registration or Dental Cleaning goes at the top. Scroll down to Pick up Cat Food/Detergent/Milk and Buy New Laces for Running Shoes. At the bottom is where you want to put the stuff that you'd like to do, but if you never get around to it, no one will notice: Clean Grout Around the Bathtub, for instance.

◉ **How do you figure out priorities?** Here's what I do. I look at the items on the list and I ask myself what good or bad things will happen if I do or don't get them done. Like, if I don't hand in a homework assignment on time, I know I'll get a lower grade. Bad thing. If I get my homework done and I can afford to take time out for a movie, good thing. You get the idea?

◉ **Here's a hot tip:** finish one task before you go on to the next. In other words, if you've prioritized your to-do list like you should have, you don't go on to the number four priority until you've got number one squared away.

## Remember These for Your "Don't Forget" List

The more you make lists, the more natural it becomes. Soon, you'll find yourself really getting good at it and you'll be amazed at how much time you save.

◉ **Check off your to-do list** as you go along. Or better yet, put a big red line through each item. It feels good to check those little buggers off and to see how much you got done!

▣ **Not only are to-do lists** valuable, but now that I use a real organizer, I see how much other great stuff is there at my disposal. My organizer, for instance, has an insert that helps me keep track of expenses, and my girlfriend uses one of those electronic organizers that practically runs her life.

▣ **I got so good** at keeping a daily to-do list that I figured I'd start thinking bigger, and so now, I keep a weekly to-do list, too. This way, I can try to organize myself for bigger chunks of time. If I have a project due ten days ahead, I can see it coming on the horizon. Next step is the monthly list!

▣ **The same way** that I prioritize my daily to-do list is how I prioritize my weekly list. For example, I tell myself that I can only watch three hours of TV a week, no matter what. Or, this week, let's say, I only have time to go out one night on the weekend.

▣ **One thing you should know** about to-do lists: they're kind of like New Year's resolutions in the sense that you make up this list but very few of us do all the things that are on these lists every day. We're only human and most of us run behind now and then. If you do, don't make yourself crazy, and whatever you do, don't make those around you crazy. Just put the unfinished items onto the next day's list, if it still makes sense to do so. But keep in mind that you shouldn't just add on to tomorrow's list and end up

with 13 or 14 to-do items rather than a manageable
nine or 10.

# The Lost and Found of Time

If, over the course of the next few weeks, you keep
close tabs on how you use your time, our guess is
that you'll be shocked by how much of it slips
through your fingers. All of us can save hours a week
just by becoming aware of certain little shortcuts and
"fast ones" we can pull on old Father Time.

There's no end to the ways you can save time
when you start paying attention to it. The following
tips will give you some ideas of ways to own your
time again in the many areas of your life.

## Shopping

Being a smart shopper is a necessity these days, when
time is tight and prices are high. Check out the following ideas.

◙ **I keep a shopping list** with a pencil on a string
on the refrigerator door. Whenever I use something
up, I write it on the list. When I go to the store with
my roommate, we tear the list in half and we meet
back at the checkout, having done the job in half the
time.

◙ **My trick** when it comes to shopping is to always
shop in the same supermarket. Supermarkets today

are so huge that if you go to a new one that's unfamiliar, it will take you three times as long. When I go to the same one all the time, I know exactly where to find the onions, light bulbs, toilet paper, cat food, and so forth.

◙ **If I'm shopping** and I see something I love, like a blouse that's really right for me or whatever and that's not going to go out of style, I'll buy two, if I can afford it. I know that when one wears out, I'll still have the other and I won't have to spend the time to go out shopping for the perfect blouse.

◙ **I do a lot of shopping** on the Internet. I get great prices and I don't have to drive to a mall and look for a parking place. A lot of the stores you go to in the mall have Internet sites with special Internet bargains, too.

## Cooking

Don't let cooking "eat" up your time. There are too many great shortcuts available these days. No one needs to get bogged down behind the stove. Here are some ideas we've collected for you.

◙ **Double quantities when cooking** whenever you can. If you freeze away the extras, you'll have two or three meals for the "time price" of one.

◙ **If you're planning** to grill a steak or other meat, let it stand at room temperature for about an hour first. It will cook faster, brown more evenly, and will stick less to the pan. But don't try this with ground meats or organ meats like liver: they're too perishable.

🔳 **Everybody should know** about the garlic and ginger and chilis that come in a jar. Not the powdered spices, but the actually chopped up stuff. These really save a lot of time.

🔳 **This will only save about a second**, but a second here and a second there adds up. You don't need to rinse cooked pasta, no matter what anybody's told you. In fact, rinsing dries it out. Just dump it from the colander to the bowl and proceed with the sauces.

🔳 **I always line the pans** I use for roasting with foil. Instant cleanup!

## Around the House

Let's face it: cleaning is a drag. Here's how to make it go faster and better.

🔳 **I'm the president** of the international "I Hate Cleaning" society. The same way I prioritize my to-do list is how I prioritize my housecleaning. I figure out what needs to be done on a daily basis (picking up dirty clothes from the floor), on a weekly basis (cleaning the bathrooms, throwing out garbage, a little light vacuuming), what needs to be done monthly (I don't know, changing the linen?), and yearly (Turning the mattress? Washing the windows? Yeah, right!).

🔳 **I keep cheap handheld vacuums** on every level of the house. I hardly ever take out the vacuum except maybe if company is coming.

🔳 **One of the things** that used to eat up a lot of my time was looking for stuff. Scissors, scotch tape, screwdriver; everyday stuff like that. Then I had this brainstorm. I could buy four screwdrivers at $.99 apiece and I could keep them in strategic parts of the house. Same for scissors, tape, and all those other little things I was always misplacing. It's great!

## . . . And About That Microwave

Many people today, particularly students, live by the microwave. Microwaves are great, but too many of us choose to believe that they don't need to be cleaned. How grungy is yours? We thought so. Try the following:

* Before you clean your microwave, put a measuring cup of water inside, bring it to a boil, let it sit a little, and then clean. The moisture given off will make it much easier to wipe off dried-on food.

* Keep a little dish of baking soda in the microwave between uses. This will absorb odors so that your baked potato doesn't wind up tasting like bacon and vice versa.

* Have you ever experienced the horror of microwave popcorn nuked to utter blackness? What a smell! Eliminate it by mixing equal parts water and vanilla extract (the less expensive imitation vanilla will do), bring it to a boil, and then keep the microwave shut for 12 hours or overnight. And remember not to char your popcorn next time.

# Laundry

Another of life's tiresome duties. Here are some ways to get around it.

🔲 **I hate losing socks**, so now I just wear white and black socks, all the same style, so I can mix and match.

🔲 **Go home to your mother** with your laundry. It's good for you, it's good for the relationship.

🔲 **Do your laundry regularly**. If you let it pile up, it gets totally overwhelming and a nothing little job suddenly has become this ridiculous mountain of clothes you have to deal with.

---

## Stain Removal

Stains are a pain. Dealing with them takes time. Here are some shortcuts to know about.

✳ If you've done a load and the colors have bled all over the place, *don't dry the clothes*! First, try washing them again with a colorfast bleach. If that doesn't work, take the damaged item and treat it with color remover from Rit®, the people who make dye. It's really effective stuff. And next time, separate your whites from your colors!

✳ Use peroxide on blood stains.

* For gum that's adhered to your clothes, brush on some egg white with a toothbrush, let it sit for 15 minutes, then wash it.

* I use rubbing alcohol on ink stains. It works in most cases.

* For spaghetti stains, wet the fabric and then sprinkle some powdered dish detergent on the stain. Scrub it gently with a toothbrush, then rinse and launder it.

* Permanent marker stains don't have to be permanent. Try covering the stain with sunscreen, then rubbing it off with paper towel. You may have to repeat a bunch of times, but it just might work.

## Home Maintenance

▣ **Silhouette your tools** on a pegboard so you'll know just where everything goes.

▣ **If you're always in a panic** looking for warranties and appliance manuals and stuff like that, do what I did. Get a three-ring binder, punch holes in those important papers, and keep them all together where you will always know where to find them.

▣ **It's a little thing**, but it makes me crazy: the amount of time it takes to untangle stuff like electric cords, Christmas tree lights, garden hoses, and whatever else has the capacity to get tangled. Now, I put everything like that on reels and it saves me a lot of grief.

## Travel

🔲 **I like to keep** an extra cosmetic bag packed just for travel so it's always ready to go.

🔲 **If I can**, I get foreign currency ahead of time.

🔲 **Consider using a travel agent** to make travel plans. Chances are, it won't cost you any more and you'll save tons of time not waiting on the telephone to talk to some person at an airline.

## Miscellaneous Time Savers

🔲 **I try to cut down** on all unnecessary trips. For instance, if I'm out shopping and my gas tank is still half full, I'll fill it anyway so I won't have to make a special trip at some other point just to get gas.

🔲 **Have you discovered** automated banking? It rocks!

🔲 **Make the best use** of your commute. If you're in walking distance to work, walk the walk and make this into your exercise time. If you're sitting on a bus or a subway, you might take this time to learn a new skill—knitting, the rules of bridge—or you might further organize your to-do list or catch up on some much-needed sleep. If you're driving, check out Books on Tape. You can learn so much about so many different things while you're stuck in traffic.

◙ **A bowl of coins** goes a long way toward commutes, tolls, school lunches, money for a newspaper, and so forth. Make a routine of emptying your pockets into the bowl at night. It beats picking up pennies from the floor when you take your pants off.

◙ **Buy a phone answering machine** if you don't already have one. That way, you can monitor incoming calls and decide when and if you want to take them. For instance, if you come home and you need an hour to be by yourself, you can get back to your aunt at some other point. She'll understand. Another option is to consider getting rid of your answering machine. That way, you'll never have to return a call!

◙ **Carpool** whenever you can. It's insane to live any other way.

Okay, now that you're handling stress, feeling organized and motivated, and are working on sprucing up your study skills, let's move on to another very important subject: getting along with other people.

## Chapter 8

# Works and Plays Well with Others

**C**an you remember back to elementary school when you were graded on "Working and Playing Well with Others?" What were you? Excellent, good, satisfactory, or unsatisfactory? Well, guess what? Even though your current report card may not evaluate your interpersonal skills, you can rest assured that you are being judged on them, every day of your life. The people around you—your teachers, fellow students, your boss or manager or coworkers, your family and friends—they are all judging whether you are excellent, good, okay, or not so great at getting along with others. And the grade you get may well predict your ultimate success in school and beyond.

When you think about how you interact with other people, first think about what kind of personality you project to the world. Some of us are blessed with warm, sunny personalities that just naturally make people gravitate to us. Others may be strong natural leaders who can easily convince friends and associates to do things their way; such people are sought out and sought after, whether the context is professional or social. Then there are those who are quiet, reserved, or even seriously shy. Entering a group situation for such people always requires a certain amount of "rehearsal." The interactions of such people are rarely spontaneous, but even so, they can still be successful and satisfying. Still others among us have significant problems fitting into a group altogether. Such people may be argumentative, hypercritical, sarcastic, suspicious, quick to pass judgment, ungenerous, even mean-spirited or downright destructive.

Where do you see yourself fitting into any of the above characterizations? To answer that question, you're going to have to look at yourself as objectively as possible. You may want to solicit the opinions of friends and family in order to help you make an assessment. It is only when you begin the work of serious self-assessment that you can start to make the changes necessary to help yourself function more effectively in group situations.

As a student, think about how important it is for you to be able to interact with others. You have to be able to work well with a teacher—an authority figure—in order to do your best. That teacher has to respect you and you, hopefully, will respect that teacher, for it is in an atmosphere of mutual respect that learning can most easily take place. You will have other authority figures to reckon with: a principal, a vice-principal, a guidance counselor, coaches. What about other students? Not only will you be thrown in with them socially, but also you'll need to rely on them as lab partners, in group projects, and so on. You may be in a dormitory setting where you are sharing space with one or more other students, trying your best to coordinate your lifestyles. That might not be so easy, either.

Personality is a complicated issue, but fortunately, we can all learn new and positive ways to interact with each other. In this chapter, your fellow students will share some of the many ways that they have improved their relationships with specific attention paid to such matters as communication, conflict resolution, and more.

# The Fundamentals of Communication

All relationships start with communication, though not necessarily spoken communication. In the beginning, an infant communicates with his or her mother in nonverbal ways. As a child gets older, hopefully he or she will understand the give and take of ordinary conversation: when to talk, when to listen. Wherever you are, wherever you go, you'll find that communication is central to the human experience. If you cannot make your wants and needs known, or if you cannot be receptive to the wants and needs that others express, then you're going to have a hard time being part of a team. And keep in mind that your ability to be a part of a team may prove a crucial factor in determining your ultimate success. If you're a loner who finds communication painful, maybe you'll want to go into some field where you rarely have to talk to other people like being a lighthouse keeper. But if you're a lawyer or a doctor or a teacher or a plumber or a waiter or a secretary or a flight attendant or just about anything else, communication is going to come into play, so you might as well start thinking right now about how you can get good at it.

▣ **You know**, when you come down to it, everything is about communication. It's not just your words. The expression on your face, the way you make eye contact, and your body language all telegraph messages just as fast, if not faster, than words do. So if you want someone to get a message—or maybe even more important, if you *don't* want someone to get a message—you need to be aware of what your body language in saying. Folding your arms in front of your chest or slouching in your chair are statements that can be more powerful than a thousand words.

▣ **People from different cultures** communicate in different ways, and as our society becomes more and more multicultural, we all need to be aware of those differences. For example, in some cultures, if you look down at the floor when you're talking to someone, it's taken as a sign of respect. In other cultures, if you look down at the floor when you're talking to somebody, people are liable to think that you're shifty or that you've got something to hide.

◉ **Some people** have absolutely no idea of what's considered an appropriate distance between two people who are having a conversation. They'll put their faces really close to mine and that drives me crazy. Haven't these people ever heard about "personal space?" I once read somewhere how it's normal for family, lovers, and close friends to stand about a foot apart from each other, while everyone else should keep four to 12 feet apart. Sometimes I want to carry a sign around with me that says, Stay Behind the Line!

◉ **Just as important as your words** is your tone of voice. If you're loud, if you're a "low talker," if you talk too fast for people to follow your train of thought: all of these are problems in communication. Ask your friends to critique your tone of voice. Does it need softening? Strengthening? Slowing down? Speeding up? Do a lot of people say, "Excuse me?" when you're talking to them? If so, you have work to do, but the good news is that if you do the work, you'll start seeing improvement in your communication in a matter of weeks.

◉ **When it comes to communication**, the environment can have a big impact on what goes on. I know that when I find myself in a big group scene, like a party or whatever, I have a really hard time screening out what's going on around me. My attention wanders and I've wound up really alienating people who think I'm looking around for someone more interesting to talk to. But that's not the case at all. I just have what's called "selective attention," but I'm working at getting better at this.

---

## What Is Your Communication Style?

In Chapter 5, you read about the different learning styles: visual, auditory, and tactile/kinesthetic. Similarly, there are different communication styles. Some of the more popular styles include the following:

**✳** *The Salesperson.* This communicator likes to touch and feel and talk. It's a very direct, open style, with little reluctance in approaching strangers.

**✳** *The Thinker.* This communicator may be quite reserved, even guarded, but with excellent problem-solving abilities that will always make him a welcome member of a group.

**✳** *The Relater.* This is the sort of person you can turn to and confide in, who interacts warmly, and who genuinely seems to care about other people.

Of course, there are many other types. Look around your classroom and see if you can name a "type" for each of your fellow students . . . and for yourself!

# Personality and Attitude

In discussing interrelationships, it is important to make a distinction between personality and attitude. Personality is that deep, instinctive part of a human being that is difficult, if not impossible, to change. Someone with a quiet, shy, introverted personality is unlikely to turn into a joke-cracking, back-slapping extrovert, and there is no reason why someone should strive for such a transformation. Introverts can have very positive feelings toward other people, can form excellent relationships, and can enjoy a life that is just as satisfying and successful as that of an extrovert. Different strokes for different folks, right? As for attitude, let's think of it as a kind of worldview, influenced or even formed by our environment and representing all the things we take away or possibly reject from our parents, teachers, peers, even books and movies. A person's attitude might be characterized as accepting, collaborative, haughty, critical, withdrawn, overbearing, or any number of other things.

Personality and attitude go hand in hand, sometimes reinforcing each other, sometimes causing conflict. You might have an introverted personality but might also care very deeply about other people. Such a combination might lead you into a career as a social worker, let's say, or a physical therapist, where a caring attitude counts and an introverted personality will not necessarily hold you back. On the other hand, you might be an extroverted person who does not really care all that much about other people. This combination of personality and attitude might not be a problem if you go into an area like sales, for instance, where you can enjoy success even while achieving only superficial relationships with many people. But it could prove a problem if you go into an area like teaching, where you would really need to have a more positive attitude toward people to do your job well. While we may not be able to change the personalities that we are born with, we can certainly change our attitudes through disciplines like assertiveness and reframing, and by being open to receiving feedback and even criticism. Let's hear from some who have done just that.

## New Ways of Thinking

Why get stuck in the "same old, same old" thinking patterns? Try on some new ways of thinking that may lead to new ways of "being."

◙ **My soccer coach** tries to work with us on assertiveness. He says it's a three-step process, with the key phrases being "I feel . . . I want . . . I will." For instance, you might say, "*I feel* I'm being taken advantage of in this situation." Then you step back and ask yourself a few questions about what the situation really is and what it is you really want, and maybe you'll come up with something like, "*I want* to be recognized for all the work I do." Finally, you get into the action mode: "*I will* make it clear that I'm not going to allow myself to be passed over again." It's like the 1, 2, 3 punch, and it's a pretty effective way of organizing yourself.

◙ **Assertiveness** has never a big part of who I am. I'm not alone: I think a lot of women have trouble being assertive, particularly women in my family. But I do think that once I get out into the world, where so many demands are being made on me, I'm going to have to learn how to get better at it. If I don't learn how to say "no," I'm going to be in big trouble.

◙ **My sister** is a substance abuse counselor, so she has a lot to say on the subject of attitude. She talks to her clients about "reframing." When you reframe, you adjust your attitude by essentially changing the meaning of an event. For instance, your teacher might say something to you like, "I think you can do better." Now, you might have a gut reaction to that where you're telling yourself that you've been put down bad and you're fuming. Reframing, however, gets you to put the brakes on those feelings. When you reframe, you might say something like, "My teacher's right. I could do better. And next time I will. Next time I'll really nail that assignment." Reframing slows you down so that you can turn any experience into an opportunity to learn.

◙ **My grandmother** was a real lady and she always said there was something we kids needed to learn: tact. You don't have to say everything that comes into your head, she'd always tell us. You can say it straight and be totally honest without being harsh or critical.

## Feedback and Criticism

Hearing the truth about yourself can hurt. But once you get beyond the hurt, you can use this input to make important changes.

◙ **Part of having a positive attitude** is being able to handle criticism. My father was always very critical of me, so criticism was something I saw as a very negative thing, and I've had to work really hard to get better at accepting it. I used to withdraw or rationalize or try to blame other people whenever I was criticized, but now I've come to learn that the best way to handle criticism is to see it as a positive thing. It's feedback that can teach me how to become better at what I'm trying to do.

◙ **Too many people**, when they're criticized, rush to their own defense. I don't think that's such a great idea. If your teacher tells you you're not really focused, for instance, I don't think you should turn around and start telling her how you really are focused. I think it's better to say absolutely nothing and just listen. Later, after you've had a chance to reflect, then maybe you'll want to make a few points. But don't skip the reflecting part.

◙ **I always go for** the "second opinion." For instance, if a teacher says to me, "You're disorganized," I'll take a survey of my friends and family. "Hey now, listen up," I'll say. "Am I disorganized? Have you noticed this about me? Just how disorganized would you say I am?" It's a reality test, and even if it hurts, it's important to do it.

◉ **Giving negative feedback** can be just as hard as getting it. Our English teacher makes us critique each other's papers, and in the beginning, I was really uptight about telling people things that I didn't like or that didn't work for me. But our teacher gave us good guidelines. She said we should only criticize people on what they could work at changing. If someone is clearly not a genius, it doesn't do any good to say, "You know, you're not very smart." But things like organization and clarity and backing up your points are things that we can all learn to improve on, to some degree or other.

## Anger Management

If you haven't mastered certain interpersonal skills like assertiveness, then you probably will find yourself in situations where you feel angry and you're not sure what to do next. Even if you have learned to become assertive, there may still be times when your anger feels like it could veer dangerously out of control. Some people deal with anger by repressing it. Maybe they'll get a headache or become constipated or do something that is harmful to their own bodies. Other people will deal with anger by displacing it. They have a run-in with a teacher and then go home and pick a fight with their little brother or kick the dog. Still others may walk around with anger until it builds up into rage, and then the rage comes out in wildly explosive and highly inappropriate ways. We've all heard of road rage and airport rage, and the outcome of those reactions can be frighteningly intense and even, in some situations, tragic. So how do we manage our anger in ways that are effective? Here are some thoughts from your colleagues.

◉ **Anger** is not something you have to be afraid of. It's just a normal part of life. In fact, being afraid of it can be exactly the thing that sends it out of control. You want to be familiar enough with your anger and comfortable enough to be able to take your "anger temperature." Ask yourself, "How angry am I? On a scale of 1 to 10, am I a four? A seven? Am I off the charts at 11?" If the answer to that last question is "yes," then you're going to have to be able to take emergency action to make sure that you're not going to do something you regret like play bumper cars in the parking lot. Some actions, once they've been taken, cannot be undone, and the consequences can be life-changing, both for you and for the object of your anger.

◉ **You know that expression**, "an ounce of prevention is worth a pound of cure?" It makes sense when you think of it in terms of anger. I try to prevent fights by avoiding those things that I know are going to set me off. Like I always used to have a fight with my brother when we'd play ping-pong because he's so incredibly competitive and such a sore sport if he loses. So now I don't play ping-pong with him anymore. If I want to do something with him, I'll suggest we watch something on TV or whatever, something where winning doesn't come into play.

◉ **If I'm really in a rage** over something, what I'll try to do is to make myself breathe deeply. Putting oxygen into your body is definitely the right direction to go in, but you've got to make sure that you're doing deep breathing. That means breathing with your diaphragm, bringing it up from your gut. Shallow breathing isn't going to help anything. Counting to 10 when you're angry can also help. It may be a cliché but the idea is to give yourself some space, and the time it takes to count to 10 may be just what you need to keep yourself from saying the first stupid thing that comes into your head.

◉ **I try to stay away** from certain "hot-button" words like "Never" or "Always." Those are the kinds of very charged words—"You never do anything right"; "I'm always waiting for you"—that only make things worse.

◉ **Humor or just plain silliness** is to anger what a pin is to a balloon. It just takes the air out of it. I'll stick a comedy movie in the VCR when I'm angry and I'll feel better. Watching someone in a slapstick comedy is just what I need to get me out of a really bad mood.

 Conflict Resolution

Regardless of how positive your attitude is and how sunny your personality may be, there will doubtless be occasions when you come into conflict with other people. That's just the way things are. How you handle and resolve conflict will have a lot to do with determining your ultimate success in school, in a job, and in life in general.

◙ **I try not to take things** so personally. Sometimes, people are having a bad day and you just get hit by some flak. It doesn't have to be such a big deal all the time. Suck it up and move on.

◙ **If somebody says something** that I feel I have to disagree with, I always start with the word "I," not "You." In other words, I put the action in the context of how I feel about it. Like, instead of saying to a friend, "You never listen," I might say, "I feel like you don't hear me." Or instead of saying to a teacher, "You're going too fast," it's a lot better to say, "I'm having a hard time keeping up." You see the difference? And I always stay in the present. Always. Never bring up a whole history of who did what to whom. Once you start doing that, things will spiral out of control.

◙ **When wolves get into a fight**, one of them makes itself submissive and shows its jugular to its enemy. This display usually puts a stop to the fighting. I learned from wolves. When I'm in a fight, I'll say something to the other person like, "You know, I really feel I could use your help to figure a way out of this mess." When I do this, the other person usually rushes to help me and I never feel like I've lost face.

Quite the opposite. I feel like I've figured out a way to manage the situation.

🔳 **Never say or do anything** in haste and never, ever, write anything down! I think one of the worst inventions known to mankind is e-mail in the sense that too many people, when they're angry, will go to their computer and jot off a furious note. Well, that e-mail becomes an historical record of your anger that you would rather not see again when you're feeling better. Use self-control in all your dealings and don't shoot off (or write off) at the mouth!

🔳 **Before, after**, and, if possible, during a conflict, I'll try to share a good feeling with the other person. I'll figure out something good to say about her. That way, I can acknowledge that there's a problem but I put the problem in the context of something bigger. For example, I might say something like, "Jean, you always say what's on your mind and I admire you for that. But I'm not sure you understood me correctly, blah blah blah." You see? It's a little dance. A give and take, which is a far cry from going in with both barrels and trying to blast a person to kingdom come.

🔳 **Go for a walk** if you're angry at someone. Breathe deeply. Eat a doughnut. Do something to break the chain of the anger. Then, when you've cooled down a little, ask yourself what you're looking for. For some people, it's an apology. The apology becomes like this pot of gold at the end of the rainbow. I try not to be so focused on apologies because some people will never apologize. It just goes against their grain and if you establish that as a condition, then you may never get over the anger with them. So, instead of looking for apologies, I try to focus on co-existence instead.

---

### Dealing with Teachers

Maybe you were intimidated by teachers or resentful of their authority at some point in your life. Don't let yourself get hung up on such feelings now when you need to be as positive as you can to ensure your success. Here are some pointers from your fellow students about ways to make sure your relationships with teachers are good ones:

* Make personal connections with your teachers, as it is natural to do so. Talk about your interests when you can. Maybe you'll find that your teacher also loves horror movies or cats or sushi. That's a nice easy way to connect.

* Participate as much as you can. It's hard work to teach to a class of stuffed owls. Teachers are very grateful to students who meet them halfway in terms of classroom discussion.

* Remember that teachers are people, too. They have good and bad days, just like anyone else. If they seem short-tempered or irritable, don't take it personally. Let it roll off of you.

---

As we said at the top of this chapter, the personal interactions we have with other people may very well determine whether or not we'll ever be able to achieve real success. Again, it is important to remember that the ability to get along with other people is a skill that can be learned, even if some of us are born with people skills that come more naturally than others. A vital part of communication that is essential to good interrelationships is listening. Let us look at listening in more depth in the next chapter, where we will find out more about how to present ourselves to the world and how to project a good image.

Chapter 9

# SAY IT AND HEAR IT

If we had to name one skill that every student absolutely has to master, that skill would be listening.

*Did you hear what we said?*

Listening, unfortunately, is becoming something of a lost art in our society. In the centuries that came before the 21st century, people were taught the basics of communication. Young men and women courted each other in a formal fashion; they were taught how to carry on a conversation in a graceful way and how to present themselves to the world so that they would maximize their appeal. In modern times, these talents have taken a back seat to self-promotion, salesmanship, and other "skills" that are supposedly geared to help you get along in a highly competitive society. As a student, however, whose job is to hear and absorb information being passed along to you by teachers and fellow students, you have to learn the communication skills you may have neglected all these years while you were watching TV, walking around with headphones, or playing video games.

Speaking, too, is a skill that you may need to work on. Certainly, you will need to make yourself understood in normal everyday conversation, but you may also be called on to present orally to your class, which is a more formal speaking situation that you will have to prepare yourself for. Public speaking, in fact, is the number one fear of Americans—it surpasses the fear of snakes, spiders, and sharks—so know that you are not alone when it comes to feeling intimidated by the prospect of speaking before a group.

But as we've said, it all starts with listening, so let us start with listening.

 Listen Up

Think about how often you are in a situation where people are not listening to you. You ask your brother to pass the butter: nothing. You ask your sister if she's finished in the bathroom: nothing. You ask your friend if he can pick you up at 8. "Huh?" he says. You repeat yourself, wondering why you always have to repeat yourself. And what about the many encounters we all have during a typical day as we try to get decent service at the places where we shop? Consider the following script, describing a customer putting in an order at a donut shop, and see if it doesn't sound familiar:

| | |
|---|---|
| *Server:* | May I help you, sir? |
| *Customer:* | I'd like a glazed donut, please. |
| *Server:* | How many donuts? |
| *Customer:* | One, please. |
| *Server:* | One powdered donut . . . |
| *Customer:* | Glazed, please. A glazed donut. |
| *Server:* | One powdered donut and one glazed donut . . . |
| *Customer:* | No! One powdered . . . I mean, glazed. . . donut. And a cup of coffee, with milk and two sugars. |
| *Server:* | One glazed donut and one cup of coffee with cream. . . |
| *Customer:* | Milk! |
| *Server:* | . . . with milk and one sugar . . . |
| *Customer:* | Two! |
| *Server:* | Two powdered donuts? |
| *Customer:* | One glazed donut! One cup of coffee with milk and two sugars. That's it! |
| *Server:* | Would you mind repeating that, sir? |

Aaargh! as Charlie Brown would say. And when that exchange repeats itself at the stationery store, the copy shop, the deli, and the laundromat, well, it all adds up to stress. Going unheard is an extremely stressful situation to find yourself in, but before you get too hot under the collar, maybe you should ask yourself how guilty *you are* of not hearing others. And why do people not hear each other? Let's "listen" to what some of your fellow students think about this.

◉ **I'm a daydreamer.** Always have been. I'm just the kind who sees castles in the sky, you know? So sometimes—actually, a lot of times—when people are talking to me, I'm off in the zone, imagining myself accepting an award or exploring a cave. One day, maybe, I'll grow up, but I'm not there yet, and that means I'm not a great listener yet.

◉ **I'm not a very comfortable person** socially. I come from a strict religious background and my brothers and sisters and I were not encouraged to interact that much with people who weren't like us. But to a large extent, I've broken away from that. I've gone off to school and I'm trying to extend my horizons, but old habits are hard to break. A lot of times, when I'm with people who seem much quicker than I am, more sophisticated and confident, I'll find myself not listening to what they have to say because I'm so busy thinking of what I'm going to say next. I realize I'm missing out on a lot by doing that, and I'm trying not to, but like I said, it's hard to break old habits.

◉ **I think the problem** is that a lot of people can't handle distractions. For instance, when I go out to eat with my mother, I'll be trying to have a nice mother–daughter conversation, but in the middle of a sentence, it'll dawn on me that Mom is not listening to me but to everybody around us. She's more interested in what the woman at the next table is telling her friend about liposuction than she is in hearing what I have to say about my history professor. "Ma!" I'll bark. "Do you realize that the only way I can get you to hear me is if I go sit at another table?" She'll get all embarrassed and apologetic, but five minutes later she's doing it all over again.

◉ **I think that one of the factors** that affects how we listen is the kind of preconceptions or even judgments that we all carry around with us. My grandmother, who's 74, tells me that when she goes into a store and asks for something, sometimes people— particularly young people like myself—pay no attention to her because they think she's old and they assume that she's got nothing to say or would just be complaining or whatever. I think that's horrible.

# Listening:
# A How-to Guide

Although listening might seem to you like one of life's instinctual activities, like breathing or swallowing, there is actually more to it than meets the eye. As we said earlier, a person can learn to become a good listener. What follows are tips from your fellow students that may help you to get better at this all-important skill.

## Listening: The Basics

No matter where you are—at a play, in the classroom, at a party—there are certain basic listening rules that apply to all situations.

▣ **Like anything else** you undertake, listening requires motivation. It demands a lot of discipline—you really have to pay attention—and like anything that requires discipline, you have to have the motivation. Take exercise, for instance. So many people drop out of it because they're not motivated enough to do it on a regular, disciplined basis. With listening, when you're about to go into a lecture, you have to give yourself a little pep talk. "I'm going to pay attention. I'm not going to look all around the lecture hall at everyone else. I'm not going to doodle. I'm not going to count the number of tiles in the linoleum floor." You've got to tell yourself you're going to pay attention because if you do, you'll get your reward: good grades.

▣ **Communication involves** a lot of nonverbal cues. People usually nod their heads every now and then to show that they're listening. You can do the same. Don't just sit there like a hard-boiled egg. Be an active listener. Nod, go "uh-huh," laugh, tsk tsk, whatever the appropriate response is to what you're being told. And ask questions. When you're really into the communication, it's like a dance. The speaker speaks; the listener listens; you ask a question of the speaker and the speaker listens; the speaker answers your question and you listen. It's so much better than just sitting there, thinking about what you're going to have for lunch.

◙ **Don't fall in love** with the sound of your own voice. Talk *to* people, not *at* them.

◙ **Always look at the person** you're listening to. That way, you can pick up on the nonverbal cues that the speaker is putting out. The pensive stroke of the chin, the arched eyebrow, the quizzical smile are all active modes of communication that you, as the listener and receiver, should be paying attention to.

◙ **One way** to let people know that you've been listening is to do this thing called "reflective listening." It's listening that reflects, or returns, the words to the speaker. Like if your father says, "Don't speed," you could say something like, "It sounds like you're worried about my driving. I drive very well. I have a totally clean record." Reflective listening reinforces what the other person has said, and in the process, clarifies the communication.

## Listening in the Classroom

Listening at a party or at a show is important, but it's not going to make or break you if you miss something. Listening in class, however, demands much more concentration, and much more is at stake.

◉ **Sit right up front** in the classroom. So some people will think you're a suck-up; big deal. The closer to the teacher you are, the more you'll be able to hear. Also, the better you see, the more you can hear because it's easier to listen to someone when you can see them. You'll also form more of a relationship with your teacher that way, which doesn't hurt either.

◉ **If you're like me**, your teachers probably told you not to fidget when you were young. The thing is, though, that fidgeting—or at least changing your body position—helps me refocus when I'm tired from all that listening. And I do get tired, because listening is hard work.

◉ **One thing** you absolutely have to keep in mind is that you're not going to be a great listener if you're trying to get by without enough sleep. You could be hearing President Lincoln deliver the Gettysburg Address but it wouldn't make a bit of difference if you got in at five in the morning and here you are now, sitting in an eight o'clock class. If that's the case, your head's going to hit the desk no matter what you're listening to.

◉ **One thing is for sure:** you'll listen better if you're intellectually engaged. I hate how so many of my friends are always talking about how bored they are. Bor-ing! Bor-ing! It's such a bor-ing thing to say. If you're open to learning new things, you'll find that you can listen and hear better. My history teacher gave a lecture last week about the death of the buffalo—the American bison—and some of my friends were, like, why do we want to hear about hairy cows? But I was fascinated. I heard every word my teacher said.

◉ **Listening to a lecture** is not all that different from reading a book. When you read a book, you ask yourself questions. What is the author trying to do here? Has he convinced me? Should I trust that what he is saying is fair and accurate? When you listen to someone—when you *actively* listen—you can apply the same kind of critical thinking and ask the same kinds of questions.

## Practice Makes Better

Actually practicing your hearing skills can make you a much better listener.

◉ **Try to practice listening** with your eyes closed. You'd be amazed at how much more you can hear that way.

◉ **Listening to Books on Tape** is another great way of practicing your listening skills. Check out Books on Tape from the library and play them on the way to and from school.

### Need Hearing Protection?

Check your hearing, folks. If a lot of people are telling you that you never seem to be listening to them and you feel like you are, maybe you've got a physiological problem. Even something as relatively simple to treat as a build-up of earwax can come between you and the person trying to talk to you. And don't forget: there's a lot of hearing loss among young people. If you're around loud music a lot—either as a listener or as a musician—you may already have done damage to your hearing. Find out what you need to do to protect yourself in the future at http://www.hearnet.com. This invaluable Web site, established by the nonprofit organization Hearing Education and Awareness for Rockers (HEAR), was conceived by a rock musician who suffered hearing loss.

 Speaking of...

What's the first thing you notice about a person? The eyes? The nose? Tall or short? The walk? The tone of voice? If you answered "tone of voice," you're not alone. For a lot of people, the voice is one of the most distinctive personal characteristics. A good voice can make you fall in love; a bad voice can sometimes keep you from falling in love.

Many years ago, when the movies went from silent films to talkies, there were several major stars who couldn't make the transition. Their voices—squeaky, high-pitched, or marked by sloppy diction—did not match their alluring screen presence. These poor folks had to go into another line of work or simply chose to sit it out for the rest of their days in their mansions. Surely you've had the experience of coming upon a very unfortunate match-up between a person's physical presentation and that person's voice and speech. Maybe you've met a well dressed, sophisticated-looking man who, when he opened his mouth, sounded quite different from what you perceived. Or maybe you saw a beautiful woman across a crowded room, and when you got up the nerve to go across the room to meet her, she accepted your introduction in a tone that was totally different from what you thought it would be.

The voice is really very important in the way you present yourself to the world, particularly so when the connection you're making is over the telephone. There the exchange is all about the voice, and if you are calling someone to ask for an interview, let's say, and you can't make your voice sound appealing, then you're probably not going to advance to the next square in the big game called Life.

In this section of the chapter, we will hear all about speaking skills with tips from your fellow students about what's worked for them and what hasn't.

## Am I Speaking Correctly?

There are a number of elements that go into proper and appealing speech. Let's hear what they are.

◙ **I guess a good place to start** is with volume. In other words, how loudly—or how softly—you speak. Loud isn't great. You should hear my Aunt Shirley; she could blast you out of the room every time she asks you to pass the salt, but too soft isn't going to win any prizes either. No one likes a low talker. Mumbling and swallowing your words makes a bad impression. You've got to learn to project.

◉ **You know what gets me?** People who talk in a monotone. I've got a couple of teachers like that, and from the moment they open their mouths, I'm gone.

◉ **If you think** you might have certain problems in the way you speak—if your voice is too high-pitched, let's say, or too low or too one-note—you can try to improve by listening, very carefully, to the way actors use their voices. Get a tape of actors reading poetry, for instance, or, whenyou're watching a video that has really fine, trained actors in it, listen to the vocal variations that they use.

◉ **Did you know** you can add depth to your voice just by opening your mouth wider when you speak?

◉ **If you watch the evening news** and you listen carefully to the anchors, you'll see what's meant by "standard English." These people know how to modulate their voices, they know how to project, and they know how to enunciate. They don't say "didja" for "did you." They don't drop the ends of words or squash two-syllable words into one syllable. They don't say things like "I'm goin' to the liberry." But the rest of us tend to let little mistakes creep into our speech. The question is how many mistakes are acceptable?

## Commonly Mispronounced Words

Try paying attention to the way you say certain everyday words and see if you're saying them correctly. Saying them in a way that is incorrect, no matter how much you may hear that mistake being made in the circles in which you travel, can still make a negative first impression on those people you are trying to positively impress.

| Incorrect | Correct |
|---|---|
| Akst | Asked |
| Liberry | Library |
| Nucular | Nuclear |
| Drownded | Drowned |
| Famly | Family |
| Preventative | Preventive |
| Idear | Idea |
| Probly | Probably |

# Public Speaking

As we said earlier in the chapter, one of the greatest fears of the average American is speaking before a group. Now, you may never be called on to be a toastmaster at a wedding or to give an acceptance speech but as a student, you should expect to make oral presentations. If this prospect makes you sick to your stomach—as it does to so many—let us have a look at some ways to handle the anxiety and to deliver our very best in such situations.

◙ **I'd say the first rule** would be that you have to know your material cold. That means you've got to rehearse and rehearse. Put on a show in front of a mirror. Say your words out loud. Round up a few friends or family members to be the audience and encourage them to input honestly about the kind of job you've done. What they have to say may hurt, but better in a small arena than when you go out in front of your whole class and the teacher.

◙ **If you find yourself** really nervous before you go out to make a presentation, try this breathing exercise. Inhale deeply through your nose and hold the breath for a few seconds. Then slowly empty your lungs, exhaling through your mouth. This relaxes the muscles in your throat, your neck, your shoulders, and, in turn, your voice.

◙ **Start with a biggie** and end with a biggie. It's the first and last minute of your presentation that most people will remember. Don't squander it on stale jokes or hemming and hawing. Find a strong story or example or statement with which to open and close.

◙ **Don't forget your visuals.** Your audience is counting on them. Just don't talk to your visuals. It's your audience you need to be talking to. If you're using any kind of technology as part of your presentation—overheads, PowerPoint, video, or whatever—make sure that you know what you're doing. Rehearse with the equipment beforehand. Don't expect an audience to hang in there with you while you go off on a technology learning curve. And organize your handouts in advance. Make sure you've got enough and always come prepared with some extras.

◫ **It's great** if you can think up interactive things to do with the audience. Questions, games, anything to engage interest. And I like it when the presenter moves around the room instead of staying in one spot. It breaks up the monotony.

◫ **Unless you have reason** to think otherwise, assume that the audience is on your side and is rooting for you. And don't feel that you have to apologize for your mistakes. If you start apologizing for leaving something out, let's say, you may only be drawing the audience's attention to something they might never have noticed in the first place.

## It's a Gesture

What is a gesture? It's a physical movement that is meant to enhance what you are saying. Some people, when speaking before a group, simply have no idea what to do with their hands, and their awkwardness around this issue intensifies their general nervousness. Here are some pointers about how to effectively use gestures:

* Don't keep your hands in your pockets. It will look like you don't know what to do with them, which, to be honest, is why they're in your pockets, isn't it?

* Keep your arms to your sides when you're not making any gestures.

* Try to keep your gestures graceful, simple, and flowing. Quick, jerky, choppy gestures will look like you're nervous and will make your audience nervous.

* Don't make the same gesture over and over again. Repetitive gestures are the physical equivalent of a monotone. Vary your gestures by switching the hands that make them, or try holding off on gestures altogether for a little while after you've been using them.

# Speaking for Non-English Speakers

Our society is becoming more and more culturally diverse with each passing year. Our schools are heavily populated with students who are not native English speakers. Learning to speak English can be a real challenge—it's not an easy language—but here are some thoughts on ways for English language learners to improve their speaking skills.

▣ **In school**, use as much English as you can. Speak it all day long. Maybe when you get home you'll be speaking French or Spanish or Portuguese or Swahili or Chinese, but in school, your first choice should always be English. And don't worry about your mistakes. Just get the practice you need.

▣ **A lot of big cities** have conversation clubs where foreign speakers can go to practice their English. Newspapers often have postings of them, and they're usually free of charge.

▣ **Don't hesitate to practice** your English when you go to a store or a restaurant. The service people are like a captive audience. They're there to listen to you!

▣ **Watch a lot of English language movies** and TV. It's a great way to soak up indigenous language and speech patterns.

All of the tips you've just read will hopefully prove useful in helping you achieve satisfying communications with your teachers and fellow students. In the chapter that follows, however, we will be returning to the things you have to do for yourself in order to ensure student success.

## Chapter 10

# HOLISTIC HINTS

**Y**ou don't need us to tell you how tough a student's life can be. You're working hard at the business of learning—or at least you should be, for that's the job—and more than likely, you're combining that work with some kind of part-time employment. Throw in family responsibilities and the hours you spend hanging out with friends and the balancing act gets even more challenging. You may be eating half your meals on the run and as far as sleep goes, forget about it. Being a student can sometimes feel like running a marathon and jumping hurdles at the same time, and you wouldn't want to try that without getting yourself into good shape physically, would you?

This chapter is dedicated to the prospect of getting yourself into shape physically so that you can help your chances of success as a student. It is not written for supermen and superwomen. It is written for real people with real needs who understand their limitations but wish to achieve their full potential. The tips you will find in these pages will go a long way toward helping you achieve "The Whole You."

What do we mean by "The Whole You?" Well, the idea of "wholeness" is at the heart of the word holistic, which means "to emphasize the organic or functional relation between the parts and the whole of something." Wholeness is, to our way of thinking, closely connected to wellness. Wellness acknowledges the connection of the mind and body, and is a state in which our physical, mental, and emotional conditions are all in harmony and are functioning at a high level. In adopting a holistic approach to life, we take into account the mind, the body, and the spirit, and we examine how they interact and impact on each other. To neglect one will, over time, negatively affect the other. In this chapter, we will be looking at ways to hold all the parts of ourselves together in order to stay healthy and whole. Let's start with the subject of food.

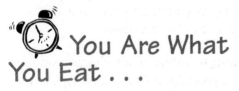 You Are What You Eat . . .

. . . is a famous old saying, and, as is the case with many famous old sayings, there's a lot of truth to it. What we put into our bodies has a great deal of bearing on how well we can expect to function. Let's hear what your fellow students have to say on the subject of nutrition.

## Water, Water, Everywhere . . .

As you probably know, 60 percent to 70 percent of the human body is water. Nothing is more important.

▣ **I'm not an expert**, but if I was to pick one piece of nutritional advice that we should all keep in our minds—or maybe get tattooed on our foreheads—it's to drink water. Lots and lots of water. Nothing is more important than keeping ourselves hydrated. Think about how much water we lose in any given day, particularly a hot day, as we sweat and what have you. Those fluids have to be replaced if we're going to keep functioning.

▣ **I've read** in a bunch of different places that you're supposed to try to drink at least eight glasses of water a day, so that's what I aim for. I don't go anywhere without my water. I always keep it with me, in a thermos, and I make a point of drinking *before* I get thirsty. Drinking after you're thirsty is a catch-up game, and depending on how much you've allowed yourself to dehydrate, catching up can be hard to do.

▣ **If you're looking to make** smart choices, stay with water when you're thirsty. Other liquids, like tea and coffee, can act as diuretics, actually causing water to leave your body. Also, why do you need the calories in colas or the chemicals in diet colas or the expense of drinking fancy juices or bottled shakes when water is so cheap, so healthy, so nonfattening, and so refreshing?

□ **I agree** with what the others have to say about the importance of water, but like everything else, you don't want to overdo. I've heard of people who were drinking like gallons of water a day, and that can be dangerous, too.

## The Basic Building Blocks

How much you're putting into your mouth is important, but just as important is what you are putting in your mouth.

□ **When it comes to food**, it's not just the food group or the amount that's important. It's the quality of the food. I always make a point of eating whole foods. Slow foods, they're calling it these days, as compared to fast food. I'm talking about foods that have the least processing. Real cheese instead of cheese food. Rolled oats instead of some sugar-packed cereal. Even a piece of semisweet chocolate if I have a sugar craving over some candy bar that's stuffed with marshmallow-nougat-brittle and that may have all kinds of artificial ingredients in it. When it comes to food, the less you mess with it, the better.

□ **Don't worry so much** about your meat intake. You don't have to eat beef, fish, or chicken for protein. Think instead about beans and nuts, tofu, or maybe a protein supplement added to a smoothie or a shake. That's what I do. Every day, I put a full measure of protein powder in a blender with some O.J. and a frozen banana, and I don't have to worry about my daily protein intake at all.

◙ **Suddenly**, "fat" has become a dirty word and that's really ridiculous. There are good fats and bad fats. The good fats, like those we get from olive oil and nuts and stuff, are really, really good for you. The bad fats, like animal fats and tropical oils (that's coconut and palm kernel oils) are bad for you. Good fats are delicious and satisfying and just a little bit of it will satisfy your hunger. When we cut down on fat, we start bulking up on carbohydrates instead, which, for most people, mean highly refined foods like sugar, pastas, and white breads. Or maybe you'll start scarfing down "lite" foods, thinking that they can't hurt you. Ha! Just watch the scale.

◙ **I just want to say a word** on behalf of fiber. You've got to make sure you have it in your diet. That means fruits, vegetables, legumes, whole-grain breads and cereals. Better do it now, folks, or you'll be paying for it later.

◙ **Short of a banana or an apple**, I don't eat anything unless I read the label first. It's important to know how much fat is in it, what kind of fat, how much sodium, if there are any calcium benefits, and so on. My friends think I'm nuts but to me it's food awareness.

## Good Eating

Hopefully, most of us learned good eating habits as children and have followed these habits throughout our lives. Unfortunately, many of us haven't been that lucky. What constitutes good eating habits anyway?

▣ **I had this sign made up**, all laminated and everything, and I stuck it on my fridge. It says, Do not eat when you're not hungry. Most of the time you're doing that, you're just trying to make up for stress, which can be better dealt with anyway by a few minutes of deep breathing or a walk in the fresh air. You'd be amazed how much easier it is to keep your weight under control when you pay attention to your stomach hunger instead of your mouth hunger.

▣ **My mother always tells me** to chew each bite of food 50 times. She drives me crazy, but as much as I hate to admit it, I can see the sense in what she's saying. I find that if I eat slowly and chew my food thoroughly, I eat a lot less and my stomach is a lot happier.

▣ **Watch your portions.** Americans are known throughout the world for eating totally excessive, gross amounts of food. The idea of "supersizing" it by ordering a 64-oz. soda is pretty much unheard of outside of the U.S. and should be unheard of here, too.

## Body Image

Closely connected to all of the important issues around food and nutrition is the all-important issue of body image. We, as a society, tend to have a warped image of what the human body should look like. While many men may be frustrated by the fact that they cannot attain the advertised abs or defined deltoids of TV stars, women have an even harder time of it. The extremely thin ideal of female beauty reinforced by television, movies, fashion magazines, and almost every other segment of the media is simply unattainable for the majority of American women. Take a walk down the street in any city or town in our nation and you'll see that there are very few size 2s or 4s out there. In fact, American men and women are getting more overweight, not less. Our eating habits and our sense of our body image both need to be addressed.

By body image, we mean the image that you see when you look in the mirror. Some people can only see their flaws and defects when they look into a mirror. Their noses are too big. They're having a bad hair day. Their skin is all lined. And, of course, they are fat. The problem with body image is that it often has nothing to do with what one's body actually looks like. The goal is to feel good about the body you have.

▣ **I've always been large.** My mother, my sisters, my aunts, my cousins, and my grandmother on my mother's side are all large, too. We're living testimony to the inescapability of genetics. I know I'm never going to be one of those 90-pound fashion models. I'm not made that way. One of my legs is bigger than most fashion models are. Is that something I should be punished for? Treated like a freak? I think I look good in clothes and know how to put myself together. In fact, believe it or not, I think I look good without clothes.

◙ **I believe** there's such a thing as a set point when it comes to weight. It's what you were meant to be. I'm 5'3 and my set point is 158 pounds. I've gone down to 128 and popped right back up like a cork. So now I feel like, "Okay, that's who I am. That's the package I come in." My friend Amy is 5'5" and weighs 98 pounds. That's who she is, and she's luckier than I am because our society values the way she looks. But to me, it's like we're two different breeds. A greyhound looks one way—long and thin—and a Labrador retriever looks another way, with thick legs and a barrel chest. Well, do you know anyone who doesn't love a Lab?

◙ **You know what I hate?** The fact that people are always talking up "will power" to me. You know, years ago, I would have died before I ate an ice cream cone in public. All I could see were the eyes on me, judging how pathetic it was for a large person like me to be eating a double dip. But do you know that the overwhelming majority of fat people do not eat any more than thin people do? Twice a year maybe I'd get a craving for an ice cream cone with sprinkles, and to go through the process of going into a scoop shop and ordering one and having people look at me was like walking through fire. Now I don't care anymore. You want to look, I say, "Feast your eyes, baby."

◙ **It took me so long** to feel okay about the kind of body I have that it makes me sad sometimes. But then I found a guy who thinks my body is beautiful and we have a wonderful time together. There were other points in history when it was considered the ideal to have flesh on your bones, not like today. Today, you're supposed to look like you're starving and haven't had a square meal in three months. So I made a decision. I was going to stop looking in the mirror every other minute and I was going to weigh myself just once a month. That's right, once a month. This business of stepping on the scale 12 times a day was really getting to me.

◙ **I have a great therapist** who suggested that what I should do is think—every day—about the qualities I have that are special. And you know what? I have them. Even though I'm very large, I have gorgeous auburn hair, lovely skin, beautiful hands, a very good mind, good friends, good taste in clothes, a sensual enjoyment of life, and I'm kind to old people, children, animals, and just about everybody else. Might as well be kind to myself, too, wouldn't you say?

◙ **I went to a workshop** on body image and they had us do this fascinating thing. They asked each of us to write down the three people in history we most admired and would like to sit down and have a conversation with. Well, everybody wrote down people like Martin Luther King, Golda Meir, Louis Armstrong, Albert Einstein, Mark Twain, Eleanor Roosevelt. Nobody wrote down Twiggy or anybody else just because they were skinny. In fact, the skinniest person on the list was Gandhi. But he wasn't on any list because he was skinny!

# Dieting

In our culture, dieting has become an obsession, a very dangerous obsession.

◙ **Diets are ridiculous.** I'm sorry. You're supposed to spend all this money buying all these products that don't work, and you can make yourself really, seriously sick in the bargain. No thanks!

◙ **Not only are most weight reduction diets** completely worthless, but so are a lot of these eating and exercise regimens that people subscribe to. If you're going to go with a program, at least ask a few important questions first like what percentage of people who enroll in the course complete it? What percent lose weight? What percent keep it off one year, three years, and five years? And what kind of medical problems result from people who have taken the course?

◙ **What's the point** of measuring out calories with sugar substitutes and little TV dinners? The real breakthrough comes when you can actually determine whether you're hungry or not, and when your body needs to eat as compared to when you're eating for all kinds of other psychological and emotional needs. When you can make that distinction, then you can start controlling your weight.

◙ **Like most people in the world**, I've been on every kind of cockamamie diet. Grapefruit, cabbage soup, some diet where I was eating steak five times a week and almost went broke. Now, I just eat with variety and moderation. I'll eat grains, fruits, veggies, a little chicken or fish, a little dairy. I cover my bases.

◙ **My little Italian grandmother** who's 89 now, still pours olive oil over everything. But she's always eating fruits and vegetables, and the way she eats meat is like a tiny little bit once a week, like a garnish on her plate. She's going to live forever, that one.

## Eating Disorders

Among young women—and increasingly among young men—there has been an outbreak of eating disorders of almost epidemic proportions in recent times. Millions are afflicted and thousands tragically die each year from them. What are these disorders and what signs and symptoms do they display?

*Anorexia Nervosa*
Characterized by significant weight loss resulting from excessive dieting, anorexia nervosa has a frightening mortality rate.

Signs and symptoms include:

✳ Weight loss

✳ Withdrawn behavior

✳ Excessive, even obsessive exercise

✳ Fatigue

* Irregular or halted menstruation

* Constant feeling of being cold

* Obsession with food and calories

* Excusing oneself from meals

* Evidence of vomiting, laxative use, and/or use of diet pills and diuretics

* Pale to pasty complexion

* Cutting up one's food in tiny pieces or picking at one's food

* Cooking for others but not eating

*Bulimia Nervosa*
A cycle of binge eating followed by purging to try to rid the body of unwanted calories.

Signs and symptoms include:

* Binge eating

* Hiding food

* Frequent bathroom visits, particularly after meals

* Evidence of vomiting, laxative use, and use of diet pills and/or diuretics

* Broken blood vessels

* Depression

* Tooth decay

* Sore throat complaints

* Muscle weakness

*Binge Eating*
This syndrome is characterized by the consumption of large quantities of food in short periods of time, with accompanying uncomfortable feelings of fullness. It is similar to bulimia, but without the purging aspect.

Signs and symptoms include:

* Weight gain

* Low self-esteem

* Depression

* Anxiety

* Loss of sexual desire

* Hiding food

All of these disorders are gravely serious and require immediate medical attention. For further in-

# Getting Fit . . . Staying Fit

Exercise. Love it or hate it, there's no ignoring it. Just look around and you'll see people running, jogging, walking, biking, swimming, weightlifting, in-line skating. Exercise is clearly a national trend. But the truth is that although the physically fit are ever more visible, we, as a nation, are becoming ever more sedentary. Makes sense, since we're a nation that year to year is becoming more overweight.

Think about the life that so many of us lead. We get up, we take an elevator downstairs, we get into a car/bus/subway, we sit at a desk for hours at a time, we work at a computer, we play video games, we watch television. Now think of the average life 100 years ago. People walked routinely to their destinations. Most lifestyles required some physical labor, whether it be shoveling snow, mowing lawns, milking cows, carrying water, or whatever. Children were outside much of the time, playing games like stickball and baseball and street hockey in schoolyards or in sandlots. Now that's a far cry from today's children who may sit for hours at a time, isolated at their computers, playing games that require only the movement of a few fingers. No wonder these children are putting on pounds from one day to the next.

It is no secret anymore that exercise is a key ingredient in keeping your mind, body, and spirit in good working order. Factoring exercise into an already busy life may not be easy, but some form of regular exercise is vital. We've asked your fellow students for a "Top 10" of helpful hints on the subject of exercise, and here's what they've come up with.

1. **Hey, you're not in this for the Olympics,** are you? You're just trying to get something good going for yourself. Something good generally means something in the neighborhood of three to five exercise sessions a week, anywhere from a half hour to an hour per session. Now doesn't that sound do-able?

2. **Lots of people hate exercise** because they think it's boring. Well, the truth is it *is* kind of boring, at least until the exercise high kicks in, which, in most cases, doesn't happen until you find your groove. I think the ticket is to pick a repetitive motion that you don't mind so much. For some people, that means walking; for others, running. Some of us like to swim while some people prefer to ride a bike (or a bicycle machine). Dancing is great for a lot of people. It's your choice. Just choose something.

3. **I always look for ways** that I can up my exercise output. Like I'll take two steps at a time when I'm walking up a staircase, or better yet, I'll walk the whole way instead of taking an elevator. When I go to the mall, instead of circling for 20 minutes looking for a parking spot that's

close to the stores, I'll park really far away and walk 20 minutes.

4. **Get yourself an exercise buddy.** Having somebody to share the agonies and the ecstasies with is worth a lot.

5. **I know that if I really want exercise** to be a part of my life, I have to do it the same time of day or else I'm probably going to be interrupted.

6. **Train, don't strain.** If you're hurting or if you're breathing too hard to be able to carry on a conversation, you may be doing something wrong. To make sure you're doing what you should be doing, check with your physician before starting any kind of exercise program.

7. **I like to track my progress.** I keep a chart of what I've done from day to day, week to week, month to month. When I'm feeling burnt out on exercise, this record of how far I've come inspires me to go further.

8. **Interval training** has been really effective for me. That means I run two minutes really fast, then two minutes slow. Then two minutes fast, then two minutes slow. Feels good.

9. **Breathe deeply**, several times a day. A lot of us run around too busy to take a deep breath. Deep breathing aerates your lungs and makes you better able to do the exercise you set out to do.

10. **You know what's a really new idea** and a good way to motivate yourself? Stop thinking of exercise as only a means to lose weight. Instead, think of it as a way to stay healthy and to feel good about the way you can use your healthy body. Large people can be physically fit, too, you know. And if skinny people don't like to watch large people dance or swim or wear a leotard, they can just leave the room.

## And Then There's Sleep

Of all the subjects we've talked about so far—nutrition, body image, exercise—none is more important than the issue of sleep. Sleep is that blissful-for-some/trouble-for-others behavioral state character-ized by little physical activity and virtually no awareness of the physical world. Scientists don't know why humans need to sleep; all they know is that they do and that it is entirely necessary. Research has shown that after as few as six days of reduced sleep (four hours or less a night), the body is limited in its ability to metabolize carbohydrates. In other research experiments, it has been shown that laboratory rats deprived of sleep will die in two to four weeks. Some scientists and physicians theorize that the purpose of sleep is to reduce certain chemicals that have built up in the body during the waking hours. In any case, the human need for sleep is programmed into us and the vast majority of human beings either sleep in one long snooze of six to eight hours or one longer bout of five to six hours with one shorter bout in the afternoon of one hour. The timing of sleep is profoundly connected to the cycles of light and dark. Humans are a diurnal species that chooses to sleep at night, in the dark.

Some people need 10 hours of sleep a night; others do just fine on five to six hours. Think about your own sleep habits as you hear about the sleep habits of students like yourself, and listen to the "Do's" and "Don'ts" tips they have to offer.

## Sleep "Do's"

Follow these and you'll be on your way to dreamland in no time.

▣ **I think the number one** most important thing about sleep is to stick to a regular schedule. I really got myself screwed up in high school there for a few years because I'd sleep from, like, eleven at night to six in the morning—which is fine; that's seven hours—but then on the weekend, I'd stay up till three or four in the morning and sleep till one or two in the afternoon, and my whole body clock would get screwed up. Now, I try, as best I can, to keep a regular schedule, and I'm in much better shape sleep-wise.

▣ **Naps are great.** Even 15 minutes dozing on the couch in front of the TV can go a long way. But I've been told that if you're going to get into napping, it's better to try to nap at the same time every day. Otherwise, you can interrupt your sleep schedule and wind up more tired than ever.

🔲 **Look, it's only common sense**, but I might as well say it anyway: try to relax before you get into bed. If you don't, you're just going to be lying there, staring up at the ceiling, thinking about your final exam or the funny noise in your car, so what good is that? Instead, read a book, a boring one, preferably. Have a warm bath. Listen to some nice lulling music. Give yourself a chance.

🔲 **Room temperature** is a big deal with me. I can't sleep well if the room is too cold and not a prayer if it's too hot. You've got to fiddle around until you find the right temperature and then try to be in environments that duplicate that temperature.

🔲 **If you do have trouble sleeping**, it's better if you don't get up to watch TV or turn the lights on to read. Try to stay with your normal light-dark schedule and stay in the dark, listening to music if you want. The idea is not to screw up that schedule because if you do, you're just going to have to unscrew it down the line.

## Sleep Don'ts

You could be walking around in circles all night if you're not careful to avoid these pitfalls.

🔲 **Be careful** about when you exercise. I find late afternoon is best but I'm good in the early morning, too. Just don't do it close to bedtime because if you do, you can kiss that night's sleep goodbye.

🔲 **Do I have to mention caffeine?** Stay away from it after four o'clock in the afternoon, and if you're really having problems sleeping, stay away from it altogether, at least for a while. That means coffee, tea, colas, chocolate. They're all full of caffeine. Switch to herbal teas, at least for a while. They're really nice!

🔘 **Too much to drink** too late in the day can rob you of a night's sleep. Your call.

🔘 **Careful what you eat** before you go to sleep. Not a good time for a bucket of greasy, spicy chicken wings or a pepperoni pizza.

🔘 **Don't be afraid to talk to your doctor** if nothing helps you fall asleep. A friend of mine was suffering from insomnia so he went to his doctor and she prescribed sleeping pills to help him get back to a normal sleeping pattern.

---

### Sleep Deprivation

Sleep deprivation is a serious medical condition that affects over 47 million Americans. Although it can have any number of bad effects on people, here are two of its most significant dangers:

✳ *Driver Fatigue.* According to the National Highway Traffic Safety Administration, over 100,000 automobile accidents occur each year because of sleep-deprived drivers. Research studies have shown that driving while sleepy is as dangerous as driving while intoxicated. According to researchers in Australia and New

---

Zealand, drivers who went without sleep for 17 to 19 hours operated their vehicles worse than drivers with blood alcohol levels of more that 0.05 percent, the legal limit in most western European nations.

* *Impaired Glucose Tolerance.* A study conducted by the University of Chicago Medical Center in 1999 indicated that sleep deprivation can dramatically affect the body's ability to metabolize glucose, leading to symptoms that mimic early-stage diabetes. This impaired glucose tolerance can eventually lead to actual diabetes, obesity, and hypertension.

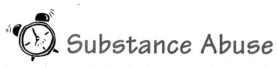 Substance Abuse

Now that we've looked at ways that people can make themselves feel good and healthy and strong and full of energy, let's have a look at ways that people go about making themselves quite the opposite. Chief among the self-destructive behaviors is substance abuse, both drinking and drug use (which often go together, by the way). How do you know if you or a friend is using too much alcohol or other substances? Have a look at this list of signs and take it from there:

* Getting drunk on a regular basis

* Avoiding others so that you can get high

✳ Giving up a lot of things that were once of interest like sports, music, drama, hobbies, and so on

✳ Lying a lot, particularly about your substance use

✳ Exchanging old friends who don't drink or use drugs for new friends who do

✳ Spending a lot of energy planning when, how, and with whom you can drink or use drugs

✳ Having a drink more to get high

✳ Complaining of hangovers

✳ Engaging in risk-taking activities like drinking and driving or unprotected sex

✳ Blackouts, when you can't remember anything

✳ Depression and suicidal thoughts or fantasies

Painful, yes? Familiar? Perhaps. Let's hear what some of your fellow students have to say on the subject.

▣ **I used to drink too much**; I have to admit it. Everyone in my family is always yelling and screaming at each other and I couldn't stand it. I drank so I didn't have to hear it in my head. But then drinking became my problem, not the noise.

▣ **I experimented with pot for a while.** Problem was, I didn't think of myself as having a problem or anything. I saw myself as a different kind of person—really different—and to me, that made it okay. Not too smart, huh?

◉ **People always see me as Little Miss Perfect.**
I'm a top student, I play varsity basketball, play the
clarinet, I baby-sit, the whole nine yards. But it's a lot
of pressure, you know? And it gets to me sometimes.
It used to get to me so much that on Saturday
nights—every Saturday—I would get so drunk. But
being sick every Sunday only made it worse.

◉ **I had a drug problem.** I admit it. And I stopped.
But the key is that it has to be *you* who wants to stop.
It's all about motivation and that's got to come from
within the person with the problem.

◉ **You can't get past a problem** like drinking or
drug use without the help of other people. You need
support, no two ways about it. You've got to get into
a program. If you don't know of any, call 1 800-662-
HELP. That's the hotline for the National Institute for
Drug Abuse and they'll help you find something in
your area.

---

### Be a Friend

Sometimes, being a friend isn't easy, particularly
when someone you're close to has a serious drinking problem but doesn't seem to know it. Can you
be the kind of friend that brings the problem to his
attention? Here are some pointers to keep in mind
if you find yourself having such a conversation:

✳ Pick a good time to have your big talk. Make
   sure it's when your friend is sober or straight,

---

and make sure you're not going to be interrupted.

✳ Talk about *your* feelings, not *his* mistakes. "Chris, I'm worried about you" is a lot better opener than "Chris, look what you're doing."

✳ Give specific examples of what you're talking about. "Remember that time, Chris, when you couldn't remember we'd gone to Jack's party?" "Remember that time when you knocked over my parents' garbage can with your car?"

✳ Watch your tone. Stay caring, not pitying or blaming.

✳ Be prepared for a lot of anger and denial on your friend's part. It's par for the course.

✳ Find out in advance where your friend can go to seek help and offer to go with him if he wants you to.

# Smoking

Everyone knows by now that smoking is a total health disaster that leads to lung problems, heart problems, bowel and bladder problems, and, of course, all sorts of cancer. So why do people do it? Because their peers do it or because they are susceptible to the intense marketing that tobacco companies are so invested in. If you're smoking, the time to stop is *now*. The good news is that half of all adult American smokers have been able to kick the habit, so there's no reason why you shouldn't be able to. Keep these tips in mind from others, like yourself, who have been slaves to the nicotine habit.

◙ **Don't start smoking** in the first place. Do yourself a favor. It's so much easier never to start than to give it up.

◙ **Switching to low-tar**, low nicotine brands is not going to make a bit of difference. The low-tar brands just make you puff harder and longer and more often to feed your nicotine habit.

◙ **The key to giving up smoking**, like giving up anything else, is motivation. You have to really want to stop in order to stop. So figure out where your motivation is coming from and write down your reasons in a place where you can refer back to them often. Ask yourself why you want to stop. Is it because your boyfriend or girlfriend doesn't want to kiss you? Because your clothing stinks? Because your teeth are yellow-brown? Because you watched your grandfather die from emphysema and you don't want the same thing to happen to you? Because it's so expensive and you can buy a CD for every two to three packs of cigarettes? Because your chest hurts when you run and you can still remember what it was like when your chest didn't hurt when you ran? Or is it any or all of the above?

◙ **You've got to realize** that stopping smoking is not going to be any picnic. Nicotine is a really powerful addictive substance and kicking the habit is hard work, nothing less. You may need to use nicotine gum, patches or whatever. Just tell yourself it's one day at a time, or one hour at a time, or one minute at a time, whatever you have to tell yourself to get through the hard parts.

◙ **If you want to stop smoking**, get some good advice about how to go about it. Your doctor or your dentist is a good place to start. You could also log on to the Web sites of some of the big organizations for directions. Try the American Lung Association (http://www.lungusa.org), the American Heart Association (http://www.americanheart.org), or the American Cancer Society (http://www.cancer.org).

---

### The Truth About Clove Cigarettes and Smokeless Tobacco

Clove cigarettes, also known as bidis, are marketed as a safe, natural alternative to cigarettes and have increased in popularity in the United States by over 400 percent in recent years. According to the December 2000 issue of *Archives of Pediatrics and Adolescent Medicine,* **clove cigarettes produce three times as much nicotine and carbon monoxide as regular cigarettes and five times as much tar.** Areas where bidis have traditionally been smoked have the highest rates of oral cancer in the world. Stay away!

---

As for smokeless tobacco—plug, leaf, and snuff—they are *not* a safe alternative to cigarette smoking. According to the American Cancer Society, smokeless tobacco can lead to cancer, increased heart rate, increased blood pressure, and mouth problems like gingivitis, gum recession, and tooth loss. Smokeless tobacco, like cigarettes, is highly addictive. Don't start!

Everything that we have covered in this chapter is important for you to know, but real wellness is an ongoing pursuit. Read newspapers, magazines, books, and listen to reports on TV and the radio about new advances in the areas of nutrition, fitness, and the other issues we have been discussing in this chapter. Now let us move on to another important aspect of your life: money.

## Chapter 11

# ALL ABOUT MONEY

Over the years, much has been said on the topic of money, but one of our favorite remarks on the subject comes from the 1930s screen idol, Errol Flynn. Flynn was famous not only for his portrayals of Robin Hood, Don Juan, and other such larger-than-life figures, but also was equally well-known for his off-screen indulgences with wine, women, and high living. "My problem lies in reconciling my gross habits with my net income," said Flynn, and we all know exactly what he meant, don't we? If only we had enough money for everything we wanted to do. If only we could discover the trick to making money. If only things didn't cost so much. Why are our feelings about money so complicated and what can we do to gain some perspective on the subject?

Generally speaking, money is a particularly pressing issue for students because by their very nature, students usually do not make a lot of money. At the same time, their education can be very costly. You don't need to be a mathematical genius to figure out where that equation leads. As a student, you may feel strapped a great deal of the time. But as strapped as you might feel in the here and now, you should realize that money is going to be something you'll have to deal with throughout your life, whether you're rich, poor, or in-between, and that makes it an ideal subject for lifelong learning. So while the overview we are about to present will hopefully serve as a good way to orient you to the topic of money, its real purpose is to inspire you to do more reading and research on your own.

## The Psychology of Money

Money is a subject that never seems to be neutral. Somehow, it always carries either a positive or negative charge, or maybe even both at the same time. As we grow up, our families give us all kinds of different messages about money:

*Money makes the world go around.*

*Money is the root of all evil.*

*Marry a rich man.*

*Get a regular paycheck.*

*Never tell anybody what you make.*

Our task, as we mature into adulthood, is to process these various and often conflicting messages and come up with something that we can feel comfortable living with. Let's see how your fellow students are coping.

▣ **Some of us** come from families where the religion is Christian, Jewish, Muslim, or whatever. In my family, our religion was money. My parents owned a couple of dry cleaners, and between the two of them, they were at one or the other 12 hours a day. The only thing they ever talked about or cared about was money. The only presents they ever gave were money. The idea of giving a doll or a little bracelet or a music box or whatever would have made no sense to them. I mean, it would have been completely beyond their range of comprehension. You give money and whoever gets it can do what they want with it, end of story.

▣ **In my family**, the worst thing you can do is talk about money. My whole life, money has been this unknowable and mysterious thing. Now that I'm getting older, I'm starting to understand that money isn't a mystery at all. It's a tool. If you know how to use it, you can get things done, simple as that.

▣ **Living in the United States** in the 21st century means living in a consumer culture. Sure, there are some people who live an alternate lifestyle and don't buy into all that, but for the most part, we're all being bombarded by advertising and credit card offers. I grew up in Turkey and it was a whole different story there. When I came to the United States, I felt like I was coming to some gigantic fair where everything was buy, buy, buy. Now that I've been here a while, I can step back a little and get a better perspective on things. Now, I try to be careful not to care too much about material things at the expense of things that are nonmaterial like nature and love and spirituality.

◙ **We live in the richest society** in history, but it's also a society where the gap between the rich and the poor is greater than it's ever been. Being rich today doesn't mean you have millions. It means having billions. In this kind of environment, you run the risk of equating material worth with inner worth. The more money a person has, the "better" or more "successful" you figure that person has to be. But being well off and being a good human being are not one and the same. The most successful human being I know is my father who's a car mechanic. He's the kind of small-town car mechanic in a dirty garage with talk radio on in the background. He doesn't make a lot of money by any standards, but he's a great success. Why? Because he loves people and people love him and everything he does is done with care and honesty. What more do you need to know?

◙ **When it comes to money**, you have to strike a balance you're comfortable with. How much of your life are you willing to dedicate to making money? How much time away from your personal life are you prepared to give up? I once read about this guy who resigned as CEO of a large company so he'd have more time for his private life. He said, "I never heard of anybody saying at the end of their life that they regretted the time they spent with their family."

◉ **My brother**, who's one of those real financial whiz kid types, says you should always have some fun with money. Even if you don't make a lot, you should take a piece of it and play with it, invest it in something and watch it grow.

---

### The Financial Pyramid

No doubt you've heard of the Food Pyramid. You probably studied it at some point in health class. Grains are at the bottom; fruit and vegetables are on the next layer; dairy and meat, fish, poultry, eggs, dry beans, and nuts are next up; and at the narrow peak, you've got fats, oils, and sweets. Well, there's such a thing as a Financial Pyramid, too, which offers a graphic representation of your lifetime financial goals. At the base are your values and goals: do you want to retire at 45? Become a philanthropist? Live in a camper? Figure it out, and when you do, construct your base. The next step represents your basic living expenses: food, shelter, clothing, transportation, and the like. Before you go on to spend money on other things, you have to meet those

---

needs. Once you've budgeted for basics, you can climb up to the next layer, Savings, Credit, and Insurance. From there, you might move on to Owning a Home. At the very top is Investing for the Future, which has to do with your children's college tuitions, your retirement, and so forth. The Financial Pyramid helps you prioritize your goals and allot your resources where they are needed most.

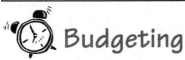

# Budgeting

Some people have an allergic reaction to the word "budget." They think of budgeting as an activity for other people, not for them. The reality, however, is that we all need to budget. Even people who make huge sums of money need to keep budgetary concerns in mind. There are plenty of tragic tales to be told of rock stars and movie stars who made wheelbarrows full of money but lived so extravagantly that nothing was left when the lights dimmed. Money can be a real stimulant, like alcohol or cocaine, and when it's new to you, you have to learn how to integrate it into your life and not become a "user." Budgeting is the tool that helps you keep your spending under control. Let's have a look at what your colleagues have to say on the subject.

## Basics of Budgeting

To get started with budgeting, you need to be familiar with the terms and the basic principles. And also the reason for budgeting in the first place.

◉ **Most people** think of budgeting as a matter of dollars and cents: what comes in and what goes out. But budgeting is more than that. The real value of budgeting is that it helps you focus on your goals. You see exactly what you need to do to reach your goal and how long it will take you. For instance, if you have $100 a month left over after all your monthly expenses, you might want to save $80 of that money each month and put $20 of it toward the sound system you've been lusting after. In a certain amount of time, you will have saved enough money to buy that system, which is different than just putting the purchase on a credit card and paying it off at 23 percent.

◉ **My dad's always after us** to save. He says that it's really a good growth thing to set your mind on something—a vacation, a couch, a car, whatever—and save for it over the long term. He says you build up a kind of discipline about your finances that's important to learn.

◉ **There are a few key terms** you really have to know if you're going to start getting serious about money. Like the difference between gross and net. The total amount of your income, collected from all sources, is your gross income. If you're working, your employer withholds certain amounts from your paycheck in order to pay federal and local taxes, Social Security (FICA), group insurance premiums, union dues, pension contributions, and other deductions. The amount of money left over is called your net income, which is, of course, less than your gross income.

◙ **If you're going to get started** with budgeting—and everyone should—you should have some understanding of what income and expenses are. Some people think of income only as your salary, but it's more than that. It could be an allowance from your parents or spouse or alimony or child support payments or welfare payments or food stamps. It could include student financial aid and tax refunds. Gifts are income. If Uncle Joe gives you $100 at Christmas, that's income. Interest earned on savings is income, too, as are dividends earned on investments.

◙ **When you're budgeting**, you have to know the difference between fixed and variable expenses. Fixed expenses don't change. Your rent or mortgage payments, your utilities, telephone, car payments, insurance payments are all fixed expenses. Variable expenses are those that come up only now and then, and are often unpredictable. If you bite down on an olive pit and break a tooth, you've got a variable expense. Your transmission goes? Variable.

◙ **My Uncle Bernie**, my father's uncle, was an accountant and he used to tell us, when he'd lecture us about money—which he did at every family gathering—that there was such a thing as the "Four A's of Budgeting." You *account* for your income and expenses. You *analyze* the situation after you've had a look at the numbers. You *allocate* your income, using it as you see fit. You *adjust* your budget as necessary.

## How To Budget

It's not hard to understand *how* to do it. What's hard is doing it!

▣ **The way to start budgeting** is to keep track of everything you spend money on, at least for a couple of months. Carry around a little notepad and jot down all your expenses: buses, subways, lunch, magazines, an ice cream cone, coffee. Whenever you spend money, write it down, with the date, and don't forget to enter the purchases you make by credit card or over the Internet. They didn't come free, you know. The idea is to step back after a couple of months so that you can study your patterns. You'll get a sense of where the money went, and you may decide to make changes.

▣ **It's easy to panic** when you first start budgeting. Even when you've been doing it for a while and you've gotten used to it, it can still get scary. The first thing to do—after you've taken that deep breath—is to look at your fixed expenses and make sure you've got the money for them. Rent, utilities, phone, insurance: there's no room to negotiate around those expenses. But if you've come up short, then you can look at your variable expenses and start chopping away. Cigarettes? Now there's a no-brainer. Instead of that double mocha latté for $3.50, how about a good old-fashioned cup of coffee for $1? If possible, walk instead of using public transportation: the health benefits are as good as the money-saving benefits. And stay away from restaurants. This is a good time to enjoy some nice home cooking. Your own!

◉ **When you get a good look** at where your money's gone and you tally up the numbers, you can start to ask some hard questions. Were your expenses more than your income? Were you able to cover all your fixed expenses? Did any sudden expenses come up? Were you able to handle them? Did you pay off your credit card balance? If not, did you at least make the minimum payment? These are hard questions and a lot of people don't like to ask them, but the longer you put it off, the bigger the hole you're digging for yourself.

◉ **I always make sure** to factor emergency money into my budget. Like if my car breaks down and suddenly I need $300 for a new ball joint, I'd rather have some emergency money put aside than have to go to my parents or whatever. I'm sure they'd give it to me, but that might mean they'd have to do without something that month.

◉ **You have to review your budget** regularly and make changes as necessary. A raise on your job, even if it's not much, is a change. Losing your job is obviously a change. Having to bail your mother out of jail is a change. When times are good, you'll want to treat yourself to some goodies: it's only natural. When times are not so good, you have to tighten your belt.

## Sample Budget Worksheet

There are many different formats that can be used for a basic budget worksheet, but here's one that we like.

| CATEGORY | MONTHLY BUDGET AMOUNT | MONTHLY ACTUAL AMOUNT | DIFFERENCE |
|---|---|---|---|
| **INCOME** | | | |
| Wages Paid | | | |
| Bonuses | | | |
| Interest Income | | | |
| Capital Gains Income | | | |
| Dividend Income | | | |
| Miscellaneous Income | | | |
| **INCOME SUBTOTAL** | | | |
| **EXPENSES (fixed)** | | | |
| Mortgage or Rent | | | |
| Utilities: Gas/Water/ Electric/Trash | | | |
| Cable TV | | | |
| Telephone | | | |
| Car Payments | | | |
| Gasoline/Oil | | | |
| Auto Insurance | | | |
| Other Transpor-tation (Bus, Subway, etc.) | | | |
| Child Care | | | |

| CATEGORY | MONTHLY BUDGET AMOUNT | MONTHLY ACTUAL AMOUNT | DIFFERENCE |
|---|---|---|---|
| Home Owners/ Renters Insurance | | | |
| Federal Income Tax | | | |
| State Income Tax | | | |
| Social Security/ Medicare Tax | | | |
| **EXPENSES (Variable)** | | | |
| Auto Repairs/ Mainten- ance/Fees Computer Expenses | | | |
| Entertainment/ Recreation | | | |
| Groceries | | | |
| Toiletries, Household Products | | | |
| Clothing | | | |
| Eating Out | | | |
| Gifts/ Donations | | | |

| CATEGORY | MONTHLY BUDGET AMOUNT | MONTHLY ACTUAL AMOUNT | DIFFERENCE |
|---|---|---|---|
| Health Care (medical/ dental/ vision) | | | |
| Hobbies | | | |
| Interest expense (mortgage, credit cards, fees) | | | |
| Magazines/ Newspapers | | | |
| Pets | | | |
| Miscellaneous expenses | | | |
| **EXPENSES SUBTOTAL** | | | |
| **NET INCOME (Income less expenses)** | | | |

# Savings versus Credit

Young Americans today are saving less than the generations that came before them and are running up higher and higher credit card debts. As an historical footnote, in the old days, many people thought that "buying on credit" was a sign of real shiftlessness and was not an option that any respectable person would even dream of entertaining. Today, most consumers buy a lot of things on credit, and there's nothing wrong with that as long as you can pay your credit card bills. The problem is that many people don't, and the carrying charges can become crippling. This dangerous situation that so many people today find themselves in needs to be looked at and remedied.

## Savings

Savings—for the proverbial rainy day—are very nice to have. It seems, however, that many of us are getting out of the savings habit, or have never gotten into it. All responsible adults should familiarize themselves with savings opportunities.

◙ **There was an old lady** who lived down the block from us. We all called her Mama Angela. She was pretty crazy but everybody loved her. She kept all her money in the piano. Everybody knew it was there but nobody robbed her because, like I said, we all loved her. But that's living dangerously. Banks are a better idea. You've got to know things, though, when you pick a bank. Like up to what amount are the deposits insured and who insures them (federal insurance, like FDIC, is a better risk than state insurance funds). What are the interest rates? How easy is it to get to your money? What types of accounts are offered? Don't be shy to ask. It's your money.

◙ **One summer**, I worked as a teller, so I know all about savings accounts. There are four basic kinds: a passbook account, which you can open with very little money but it doesn't pay much in the way of interest; a money market account with interest rates that fluctuate with the market rate, but these require a minimum balance and there are often restrictions on withdrawals; a certificate of deposit (CD) which offers the highest rates but they tie up your money for a much longer period of time; and an individual retirement account (IRA) that is used to put aside money for retirement and which carries strict penalties if you withdraw funds before you're supposed to.

🔲 **You'll discover** that the more income you earn, the more you'll need different types of savings accounts. If you're unsure about which direction to go, check with a friend or family member you trust, or set up a meeting with a customer service representative at a bank. That's what they're there for.

## Credit

The word "credit" has multiple meanings. On the one hand, it means "the borrowing capacity of an individual or a company." If you have good credit—if you own things (collateral), have paid off your debts regularly, and look like a good risk—people will be happy to lend you money. Credit also means the "contractual agreement in which a borrower receives something of value and agrees to repay the lender at some later date." For instance, if you buy a leather jacket "on credit," you may be paying it off over the course of three months. "Credit" can also mean a specific amount owed you, as in a tax "credit" you receive for overpaying. Your "credit rating" is a record of how well you've been paying off your debts and is a crucial factor in how you are assessed when you go to borrow money from a lending institution.

▣ **Getting credit in the first place** can be a challenge. I remember when I first applied for a loan, I was refused because I had no credit record. So how do you develop a credit record, I wondered, if no one wants to give you credit? It's a catch-22, right? My boyfriend suggested that I take out a small installment loan—at that time I needed a new fridge—and he would cosign the loan because he had a good credit history. As I paid off the loan for a fridge, I developed a credit history, too.

▣ **Signing up for utilities** in your own name, even though the deposit can be hefty, is another good way to start up a credit history.

▣ **Some people** just don't understand credit. They think it's there as some kind of public service, so that you can buy those leather pants you're dying to have without having to bother to wait until you save up the money for them. What these people don't realize is that anything you buy on credit will cost you more than if you paid cash for that item, probably a lot more. You have to factor in your interest charges and those can be steep.

▣ **Be very careful** about your credit rating. If you don't pay your bills, particularly your credit card bills, your credit rating will take a nosedive and you may be unable to get a mortgage or a business loan when you need to.

◉ **You should know**, if anyone ever questions your credit rating, that you have a right to see your credit record. Credit records are maintained by credit bureaus, and they can and do make mistakes. When I went to refinance my mortgage, I almost didn't get it because a credit bureau reported that I had defaulted on mortgage payments. Of course, it turned out to be a different person with the same name as me, but if I hadn't checked, it would still be following me around. For a small fee, you can see your credit record and you can find out who else has seen it in the past six months. If any of the information on it is incorrect, you can have it checked out and changed, with corrected copies sent to anyone who has seen the incorrect report.

## Credit Cards

As soon as you "come of age," you find yourself bombarded with offers from credit card companies. Credit cards can be great conveniences but they can also create serious problems. You need to have a good overview of what they're all about.

◉ **I know people** who never ever use credit cards and then again I know people who use credit cards every time they turn around. As far as I'm concerned, there's a middle ground. Your job is to see if you can find it.

◙ **Some people make credit cards** sound like the devil's work: you've got to stay away from it. That's a little extreme. Credit cards, in fact, can be very useful. For instance, let's say you live in Buffalo like I do. You're going to need snow tires to get you through the winter, right? But snow tires will set you back $300 and you just don't have that kind of money right now. But you think you'll be able to pay for it over the course of the next four or five months, so you go for it. Sure, it'll cost you more in carrying charges, but it's better than sliding off the road into a tree, isn't it? The same principle doesn't apply to cashmere sweaters, however. Snow tires can be a matter of life and death. Cashmere never is.

◙ **You need to understand** that there's a difference between a credit card, like Master Card, Discover, or Visa, which you can pay off over time, and a charge card, like American Express and Diner's Club, which you have to pay off in full each month.

## Selecting a Credit Card

How to choose? Having a knowledge base is a good place to begin.

◙ **All credit cards are not created equal.** When you've made the decision that you want a credit card, you need to shop around to make sure you get one that has the best features. Most important is the APR, the annual percentage rate, which is the interest you will be charged per year on the amount you finance.

◙ **Some cards** have astronomical APRs—up to 23%—which in this climate, when credit card companies are competing with each other for customers, is ridiculous.

◙ **Make sure** that you pay attention to the microscopic print, which details the finance charges. These explain the interest, fees, service charges, insurance, and other variables, and they differ from one company to the next.

◙ **If you pay** the minimum-only payment when you pay your credit card bill, you'll be paying the maximum amount in interest. To reduce your interest costs, pay as much as you can. For example, let's say you decide to go on a vacation to Hawaii for approximately $2,000. If your credit card has an 18.5 percent APR and you make a minimum monthly payment on that amount, it would take more than 11 years to pay off the debt and would cost you almost $2,000 more just for the interest. That almost doubles the total cost of that vacation which means you'll need another one!

◙ **Playing the catch-up game** around credit is exhausting and you really wind up the loser. If you accumulate a large balance and all you ever do is make the minimum monthly payment, then all you're doing is paying off interest without ever reducing the sum you've borrowed.

# A Glossary of Credit Card Terms

*Annual Percentage Rate (APR).*

The APR is what the credit card costs you, computed as a yearly interst rate.

*Grace periods.*

The time you have to pay before the interest is charged. There are three types of grace periods: typical, full, and no grace periods.

*Annual fees.*

Some credit card issuers charge a fee just to use their card. The fee can vary widely.

*Transaction fees and other charges.*

Some cards will charge a fee if you use them to get a cash advance, if you fail to make a payment on time, or if you exceed your credit rating. These can be punishing, so watch out.

*Customer service.*

Most issuers have 24-hour toll-free telephone numbers through which you can check your balance, make inquiries into a bill, report a lost or stolen card, and more.

Additional benefits.

Many cards offer theft protection, frequent-flier mileage, insurance, and assorted rewards, rebates, and gifts.

## Paying off Your Debt

Paying off credit card debt can feel like an endless task. Here's what it looks like

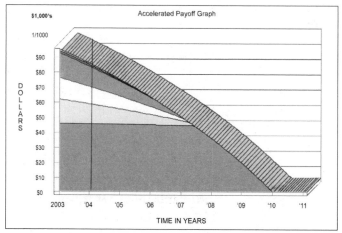

### Debt

Debt is a tough situation to be in, but keep in mind that you're not alone. Millions of Americans live with debt from year to year. In fact, it's a way of life for a lot of people, particularly for students who have to find ways to finance the overwhelming amounts of money that education costs in our country today.

◉ **A lot of debt** goes unnamed. For instance, there are some people who carry huge credit card debts but they act like that's not really debt. They're fooling themselves, and while they're doing it, they're getting in deeper and deeper.

◉ **Debt comes with certain telltale signs** you should pay attention to. Do you pay only the minimum on your credit cards each month? Do you juggle bills, skipping some to pay others? Are you gripped by panic every time an unexpected major expense comes up like a major car repair? Do you moonlight or depend on overtime to make ends meet? Do you borrow from family or friends? If any of the above sounds familiar, you'll want to make changes so that you can regain some control over the situation.

▣ **I was in huge debt** for a long time and this is what I did. I called up the credit card companies and all my other creditors and I worked out a schedule for paying off the debt. Your creditors are usually pretty responsive to something like that because they're worried, in this economic climate, about not seeing any of the money, so whatever you offer is usually listened to. Another thing you can do is consolidation: putting all your debt under one roof and working out a real plan to take care of it. If you ask around, you'll be sure to find out about reputable credit consolidation companies that can help you organize your debt payoff.

▣ **If you're seriously in debt**, get serious about resolving the problem. Contact an organization whose express purpose is to help people get out of debt. American Consumer Credit Counseling and the National Foundation for Consumer Credit are two organizations that provide credit-counseling services, either free or for a very small fee.

# Financial Aid and Student Loans

At some point or another, a great many students find it necessary to seek financial aid and secure student loans. Here is a whirlwind tour through the subject.

## Financial Aid

◉ **No one should hesitate** to apply for financial aid. A lot of students and families don't try for it because they think they're not going to get it. The truth is, there are so many factors involved in making the decision as to who's eligible that you won't really know if you are or aren't until you go through the process.

◉ **The way to get the financial aid ball rolling** is by completing the Free Application for Federal Student Aid which everyone in the world calls FAFSA. You can get the application by calling the U.S. Department of Education at 1-800-4FED or on-line at http://www.fafsa.ed.gov. Your school's financial aid office or your local public library should also have the applications.

◉ **The time to apply** for financial aid is any time after the first of the year for the following academic year. The sooner the better after January 1.

◉ **Remember**—very important—you need to reapply for financial aid every year, with a new FAFSA every year. Financial situations change from year to year, that's why.

▣ **You don't have to be a full-time student** in order to qualify for financial aid. That's a common misunderstanding. Most financial aid programs are open to students even if they're at least half time.

▣ **I defaulted on a student loan** and I figured that made me a dead duck in terms of ever getting any more financial aid. Not so. I made an arrangement with the holder of the defaulted loan and I regained eligibility. It may take some doing, but it's not impossible.

▣ **If you receive a scholarship**, make sure you report it to your school's financial aid office. Scholarships are money and they go into your overall financial mix.

## Student Loans

▣ **One of the important things**, right at the start, is to learn the difference between a Stafford loan and a Perkins loan. Those are the ones you'll be hearing about the most. The Stafford loan is a need-based government loan that's made to the student, not to the parents. The size of the loan is based on the expected family contribution and you don't have to repay it until you graduate. An unsubsidized Stafford loan accrues interest before graduating while a subsidized one does not as the government pays the interest. Like the Stafford loan, the Perkins loan is need-based, it's low-interest, it's made to the student and not to the parents, and the amount is based on the expected family contribution. Also like the Stafford loan, the student doesn't start to repay it until graduation, or if he or she leaves college or falls below half-time status. After graduation, there's a nine-month grace period during which no interest accrues. Usually, the term of repayment is within 10 years.

▣ **You can apply** for a Stafford loan after submitting the FAFSA and receiving your Student Aid Report (SAR).

▣ **A student loan** is not the same thing as credit card debt. Yes, it's borrowed money, but it's low interest and it allows you to go to college if you couldn't afford to do it otherwise.

▣ **The big questions** for a lot of people are how much *can* I borrow and how much *should* I borrow? To answer the first, check out the Federal Family Education Loan Program Guide at http://www.allstudentloan.org. As for the second, it's your move. You have to determine how comfortable you are with borrowed money. Just don't forget that it's money that has to be repaid down the line. If you don't repay it, forget about having a good credit rating.

This tour through the subject of money has been just the barest of beginnings. Again, it's up to you to keep learning. The more you learn, the better you should be able to do with your investments and with finances in general. Now, on to our last chapter: planning for your future!

**Chapter 12**

# THE JOB IN YOUR FUTURE

**H**ere you are, up to your necks in school responsibilities. You've got a lot of learning to do, exams to pass, plenty on your plate. So why are we talking to you about your future when your present is so all-consuming? Good question. And here, we hope, is the good answer: we've chosen to close this book with the subject of jobs because the truth is that it's never too early to start thinking about that time, not so far ahead, when you'll be out there looking for the right position for yourself. Maybe you've been there before, knocking on doors hoping to be hired, and maybe that was frustrating. But this time we suspect that your experience will be different. This time you've got something very solid to offer—your educational background—and while that won't necessarily assure a job, it will certainly make you more confident about your ability to perform well if and when a job presents itself.

Planning a career and looking for a job are both assignments that can feel totally overwhelming. In fact, it is perfectly normal to feel overwhelmed. Keep in mind, however, that the tips in this chapter have been collected from students like yourself who have all gone on to gainful employment. They may not have found their dream jobs right off—few do—but they're all working, making money, building up a resumé, and learning invaluable things about the world. That's what working is all about.

## Why Would Anyone Want to Hire Me?

Now that may be a painful question but it's a good one, too. Even if it's offered in a spirit of self-pity and frustration, it's still a question that everyone who is looking for a job must ask, and ask, and ask, every step of the way. For this question is, in fact, the gateway to the valuable and inevitable process of self-assessment that all job-seekers must continually go through.

One thing that is blazingly clear about the job-hunting process is that if you can't be sure of what you have to offer a potential employer, the employer won't be sure either. The thing to do is to bring clarity to the question and this you can do by self-assessment. Let's hear how your fellow students have approached this issue.

◉ **One way** our counselor explained it to us is that there are different sets of skills. One set is called foundation skills. That's like reading and writing and mathematical skills and speaking and listening skills. By the time you go out into the world to make your fortune, you should have developed a pretty good war chest of those skills, if you were paying any attention while you were in school, that is.

◉ **I have to admit** that my academic record doesn't show me to be a master of any of the foundation skills, but that doesn't mean I don't have good thinking skills. I'm a really good problem-solver, as a matter of fact. When I'm in a group that's trying to figure something out, I'm usually the one who can see a clear throughline while the rest of the group is just sitting there scratching their heads. I was on a social planning committee, for instance, and we were trying to figure out a place to have a dance. I came up with some really good ideas and I could see how impressed everyone was. Now I have to figure out how I can convince a future employer that I have that skill. I have to find a way to get it on my resumé.

◉ **I've come to realize** that I'm a creative person. One reason it's taken me so long to realize this is that nobody else in my family is creative and so there's not much of a value put on it. My parents are both nurses and they're great—I really love them—but I don't think they've got a creative bone in their bodies. But I do. I always see things a little differently than everybody else and over the last few years, people have begun to tell me that they like the way I dress and the drawings I make and how I've fixed up my room and stuff like that. I'm thinking of going into window design. I think that would be fun and I'd be really good at it. I don't know much about the field or how to get into it, but I'm going to find out.

▣ **I've been sleeping, eating**, and breathing computers since I was eight years old. It's my world. I haven't invested a lot of interest or energy in anything else and my grades in other subjects reflect that, but at least I've got some real depth in one important area, so I figure I'll be fine. Famous last words, huh?

▣ **Having been an athlete** all my life—I'm a point guard and a good one, if I do say so myself—I'm totally used to being on a team. That's how I see myself in the world. Whatever I do as part of a team. I think that's a talent you can use anywhere, and when I go looking for a job, I'm going to make sure I wind up in a place where being a team player is valued.

▣ **I've always worked.** Summers, after school; it was just a matter of course. Everybody pulled their own weight in my family; you had to. So I've been a checkout girl in the supermarket. I've worked behind the counter of a deli. I took tickets down at the movie theater. A lot of people have told me that I'm good with people. I know how to listen and give people what they want. When I get out of school, I'd like to do something in the tourist industry, maybe be a flight attendant or work on a cruise line.

# Regarding Resumés

Once you've taken an inventory of your skills and strengths the way the students above did, it's time to start putting things down in written form. That written form is called the resumé, which you'll also see referred to as a "c.v.," or curriculum vitae. A resumé is the written summary of your education and work experience, and it tells potential employers at a glance all about your achievements, accomplishments, and objectives. There are countless books and on-line sources on the subject of writing resumés and you will no doubt want to consult some of these resources that deal with this subject in detail. We only have space here for a brief overview, but even so, we think you will find it helpful to hear some thoughts from your fellow students on the subject of resumés.

## Appearances Count

It's important for job-seekers to know that the person looking at your resumé may never even get to the listing of your accomplishments if he or she doesn't like the presentation.

◉ **Rule number one:** Keep it short. One page. Nothing more. Unless you're a four-star general or whatever, you shouldn't have a problem keeping it to a page.

🔲 **Make sure** to put your resumé on good quality paper. Don't go all rainbow-crazy. You may think pink is your color or that orange is cheerful, but other people might hate pink or orange, so why risk it? Stick with white, buff, or gray. Okay, to you it might be boring, but to other people it's classic.

🔲 **Proofread!** Misspellings and poor grammar will mean points taken off. And in this competitive job market, you can't afford to lose points on stuff like that. Just ask a friend or family member to give your resumé the once-over. But make sure that person is a decent proofreader. If necessary, go back to your guidance office and draw on resources there for help with this task.

🔲 **Do not use any photographs** on your resumé. They'll make it look like the "Most Wanted" notices you see in the post office.

🔲 **Believe it or not**, some people neglect to put their contact information on the resumé and only have it on the cover letter. You can have an awesome resumé in terms of layout and the accomplishments you're listing, but if you don't have the necessary contact information—address, phone number, e-mail address—then what good is it going to do you? Make sure that the contact information is on both the cover letter and the resumé.

## And Then There's the Content

Okay, assuming your resumé is neat and attractive, the next issue is how to maximize what you've done.

◉ **When it comes to resumés**, you'll find that there's a real difference of opinion on the subject of how to arrange them. Some people arrange a resumé by listing positions chronologically while others like to arrange it according to accomplishments or abilities. Check with a librarian or on the Internet for format and then decide for yourself.

◉ **If you look at the literature** on creating resumés, it'll stress how you should always use "action verbs." You *developed, achieved, created, coordinated, maintained, formulated, introduced*, and so on. These words make you sound like a powerful force which you may very well be. And as a general rule, use simple language. Don't go overboard with all kinds of exaggerations. It'll just wind up looking foolish.

◉ **Nothing, nothing, nothing** goes into the resumé about your salary requirements. Could that be any clearer? Any talk about salary is restricted to your interview, and only if and when the interviewer brings the subject up.

◉ **Don't include personal references** on your resumé. It's safe to assume that everyone has someone who can speak well of him or her. Just list a few professional references like bosses or coworkers. If a specific job asks for personal references on its job application, than that's another story.

◉ **If nothing else**, remember this rule: *never, ever* lie on your resumé. It will come back to haunt you, and when the grapevine gets hold of what you've done, you might have really serious problems finding a job in the town you live in.

 Your Cover Letter

Even if your resumé is great, you'll still need a great cover letter to go with it. In fact, it's safe to say that nobody will even bother to look at your resumé unless your cover letter is great. So what constitutes a great cover letter? Let's see what other students say.

◉ **I'd say the most important thing** to keep in mind about the cover letter is that it should be personalized for the receiver. It's really pointless to take your resumé, create some kind of generic cover letter, and then do a blanket mailing. You'll get no responses. And never send a "Dear Sir or Madam" letter. It'll go right in the garbage. You have to customize your cover letter. Find out the name and position of someone at the company you're writing to and address it to that person. Make sure you have the name spelled right. Then talk about how you can fill the company's needs, not the other way around.

◉ **Like the resumé**, you've got to keep your cover letter to one page. That's plenty. It should basically consist of three targeted paragraphs: why you're writing (you're answering an ad in suchandsuch newspaper on suchandsuch a day or you're writing at the suggestion of a person that the receiver knows or whatever); what you have to offer (your skills—be specific—or your knowledge of a certain aspect of what they deal with); and what your course of action is (you'll call them in a week to see if you can set up a time to come by). Be proactive at the end. Don't expect to sit back and have them call you. The world doesn't work that way!

▣ **Make sure your cover letter** is on the same kind of paper and uses the same type style as your resumé, with the same kind of one-inch margins. And make sure that the cover letter, like the resumé, is absolutely free of errors. Have another set of eyes look it over to make sure.

▣ **Keep a checklist** of things to remember about the cover letter: (1) sign the letter (no one pays attention to unsigned letters); (2) end with "Sincerely" (anything else is too familiar); (3) sign with blue or black ink; (4) use a conservative stamp, not some old Christmas stamp you've got lying around; (5) type or neatly print the address on the envelope; and (6) don't staple the resumé to the cover letter.

▣ **These days**, a lot of the time you'll be electronically mailing your resumé. If that's the case, consider the e-mail as your cover letter. You don't have to put in the employer's address or anything like that: just the e-mail text will do. You can attach your resumé, but you should know that a lot of people won't open attachments because they're worried about importing viruses that way, so it might be better to paste it in. If you do paste it, have a version that's flushed to the left without any fancy type or anything.

## The Employment Portfolio

Another useful resource to develop for your job search is the employment portfolio. This is a collection, usually bound, of photos and other materials that exhibit your skills and accomplishments in your field. Portfolios may include any and all of the following:

* Diplomas

* Awards and achievements received

* Current resumé, focusing on accomplishments

* Letters of reference from former employers

* Summary of continuing education and/or copies of actual training certificates

* Statement of membership in any professional organizations

* Statement of relevant civic affiliations and/or community activities

* Before and after photographs of interesting work projects you've done

> - A brief statement about why you have chosen a career in this particular field
>
> - Any other information that you regard as relevant

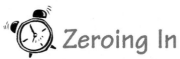 # Zeroing In

With your resumé in shape and portfolio assembled, you can begin to target those companies you think you might like to work for. Keep in mind, however, the following pointers from students who have been there.

◻ **We all hear a lot** about "dream jobs." And they are out there. But all jobs come with their ups and downs. There's the workload, the people, the commute. You have to take the good with the bad to learn what job and environment suits you best.

◻ **Let your fingers do the walking** through the yellow pages. It's a great resource. I find it a lot more "user-friendly" than the Internet, which I think is overhyped for the purposes of job searches. I do know some people who have found jobs off the net, but most people, including myself, find that it takes a long time to navigate the different sites and this time might be used more effectively otherwise.

◻ **Do we all know by now** that relying on "help wanted" ads in the newspaper is probably the least effective way of landing a good job? Many jobs are never advertised and some businesses that do advertise only run these ads because they are required to, when in fact they're really planning to promote from inside. Asking around to people you know is usually a far better route.

◉ **Networking** is a great way to find a job. It involves contacting people for information. For instance, you might have a cousin who knows someone who has a cousin who works for an ad agency you're interested in. You go through the channels and you call that person and he might be able to put you in touch with somebody else in the agency who's looking for an assistant. Presto! You've networked your way into a job possibility. Now, sometimes your networking might end up with a door slamming in your face. If that happens, just suck it up. There are people in the world who simply aren't very nice or very helpful or very sympathetic. Don't turn the behavior of such people into a personal rejection.

◉ **Your school placement office** will be a valuable resource. In a lot of cases, the school's alumni will turn to the school to look for prospective employees.

◉ **A sincere "Thank you"** counts for a great deal. If anyone has helped you, whether it was by answering questions over the phone or by meeting with you, make sure you follow up that act of kindness with your own. A brief note of thanks will stamp you in that person's memory as someone who knows how to do the right thing.

◙ **When you call a company** to make an appointment for an interview, you may be told they are not hiring at this time. If you're lucky, they may offer to schedule an interview with you anyway. Under no circumstances should you regard this as a waste of time. To become skilled at interviewing, you'll need a lot of practice, so seize every opportunity. What's more, maybe they'll have a look at you and think you're just right for that other job that hadn't crossed their minds!

# The All-Important Interview

The resumé and the networking are designed to get your foot in the door. Okay, so now that you've got that foot in the door, what's your next step?

## Getting Ready

Don't panic. Just go about your business, make sure you've got everything you need, and you'll be fine.

◙ **When you go for your interview**, make sure, first and foremost, that you have identification with you. That means a Social Security number, a driver's license, the names and addresses of former employers, and the name and phone number of the nearest relative not living with you. Don't leave home without these. You'll need them for the employment application you may be asked to fill out.

◉ **First impressions** count for a lot. That's just the way the world works. Think of how you've felt on occasions when a blind date comes to your door. Well, when you go into an interview, you're the blind date. That means your grooming and your wardrobe have to be spotless. An interview is no time for a halter top, no matter how hot the weather is, or jeans, or sandals, or T-shirts, or anything of the sort. Carry a handbag or a briefcase, never both. You don't want to look like you're moving in on your interviewer. And I'll let you in on another secret: some people hate perfume. So why risk it? Leave it off that day.

---

### Need a Wardrobe?

Many women find it difficult, if not impossible, to afford the two or three outfits necessary to project a confident and professional image when going out into the workplace. Fortunately, there are some wonderful nonprofit organizations that have been formed to address this need. These organizations receive donations of clean and beautiful outfits from individuals and manufacturers that are then passed along to the women who need them. For more information, check out these two Web sites:

Wardrobe for Opportunity at www.wardrobe.org

Dress for Success at www.dressforsuccess.org

---

◙ **Punctuality** is the number one rule. Never, ever, be late for an interview. Assume that if you're late, even by one minute, you've lost that job. To make sure you don't show up late for an interview, I advise scouting out the location a day in advance. Even if it's an hour away, make the trip and check the address. Go right up to the door so that you're not wandering around the next day in a sweat, lost in some office park when you're due for the actual interview.

◙ **Take an extra copy of your resumé** to the interview. Even if you've already sent one, the interviewer may not have it, so why get caught short?

◙ **Role-playing your interview** with friends or family can be very useful. Just make sure you're doing it with someone who knows how to take the charade seriously. And anticipate questions to use in your role-playing. Obviously, you know that certain ones are going to come up. Why do you want to work here? What do you think you could contribute to this company? You need to do your homework and make sure you've got some good responses ready.

## In the Ring

There you are, you and the person whose decision about you is going to matter a great deal. What's the key to handling this situation?

◙ **Smile.** When you walk in the door, when you leave, and whenever you can in-between. A good smile is one of the best tools in your tool shed.

◙ **Never lean on or touch** an interviewer's desk, or place your things on the desk. Some people are very territorial and you might get marks against you for this.

◙ **Hey, people**, don't use the interview as a time to have a coffee break, okay? You don't walk in with a cup of coffee or a can of soda or miscellaneous munchies. You don't smoke or chew gum on an interview. Puh-leese!

◙ **Sit up straight** and speak clearly, just like your mother told you to. And at the end, always shake the hand of your interviewer and say thank you for his or her time.

◙ **Whatever you do**, do not criticize anyone, not a teacher, not a past employer, not your Aunt Molly. An interview is not an occasion to air grievances. You'll be the one who ends up looking bad.

◙ **There will come a critical point** in the interview when the interviewer will sit back and say, "Now, do you have any questions for me?" This is not a time to sit there, looking pretty and shaking your head no. This is a time for you to seem like an intelligent, engaged person. So come prepared with a few questions. Not a whole barrage of them, just a few well-chosen ones. You might, for instance, say, "Is there a job description and may I review it?" Or "Is there an employee manual?" Maybe you want to ask what kind of opportunities there are for continuing education or if there is room for advancement. It's your call but just be sure to have some good questions handy when the time comes.

🔲 **Keep in mind** that there are certain questions that an interviewer does not have the right to ask and that you do not have to answer. Anything having to do with your race, religion, national origin or citizenship, age, marital status, sexual preference, disabilities, or physical traits are all strictly off limits. If one of these questions comes up, you should politely but firmly state that you do not think the question is relevant to the position being filled, and that you would like to focus on those qualities and attributes that are relevant. The message should sink in and your interviewer may actually wind up being impressed with your presence of mind.

🔲 **Don't forget to follow-up your interview** with a thank-you note. It's required. And it will give you the opportunity to restate your eagerness to fill the position, which could wind up being a key factor if the interviewer is choosing between two or three people.

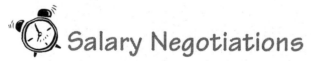 Salary Negotiations

For some people, talking about money is like a trip to the dentist: they'll do anything to avoid it. But it doesn't have to be that way. Talking about money is a completely natural part of the hiring process, and you need to learn how to become comfortable with it and good at it. Here are some tips on negotiating around money.

▣ **Do your homework.** Know what the going rate is for the position being filled. The more information you have, the more powerful your negotiating position will be.

▣ **Negotiating for a job** is not like negotiating for a car. After you buy the car, you'll probably never see the seller again. But with job negotiations, if the hiring goes through, you'll be living with the person you've been negotiating with, so it's important to operate out of good will. Keep in mind that if you're being offered the position, that means that the company you're negotiating with has made up its mind that you're the one for the job, and so you both have the same goal: to make this happen. Don't be a diva. Be a team player, right from the start.

▣ **Know your priorities.** If security is what races your motor, you may want more on the salary end and less on the commission or the benefits or whatever. If you're an entrepreneurial type of personality, you may want the reverse.

▣ **There are a lot of "extras"** that factor into a total compensation package and you need to be aware of what they are. It could be vacation time, continuing education, flex time, a six-month review with performance increases. Look into all of these and weigh them carefully when you're making your deal.

▣ **Never lie.** If you've got a job history already, never say you made more on your last job than you actually did. On the other hand, you don't have to show all your cards. In a way, salary negotiations are a little like a game of poker: a bit of bluffing may come into play. Maybe your first time doing it, it won't go as well as you hoped. But with practice, you may wind up winning a few hands.

Job-hunting can be draining but it can also be an exciting time in your life. After all, you're launching yourself on a career that can bring so much to you. If you play your cards right, the future can hold a good and stable income, interesting new relationships with people, an outlet for your creativity and energy, and a sense of purpose that makes life truly worth living. Go for your dream. You've worked hard and you deserve it.

# INDEX

## A

Activity chart, 29–30
Alcohol use, 66
American Heart Association, 192
American Lung Association, 192
Anger management, 141–143
  ways to break the chain of anger,
    145–146
Assertiveness
  in communication, 139
  stress relief, 103–105
Attention Deficit Disorder (ADD)/
  Attention Deficit/Hyperactivity
  Disorder (ADHD), 74, 79
  low self-esteem and, 6
Attitude. *See* Personality and
  attitude
Auditory learners, 79

## B

Biological clock, sense of, 82–84
Bodily-kinesthetic intelligence, 60
Body image
  be kind to yourself, 175
  feel good about yourself, 174–175
    genetic influence, 173
    the issue of, 172–173
    set point for weight, 174
    "will power," 174
Bodysmart (bodily-kinesthetic
  intelligence), 60
Brain power. *See also* Intelligence;
  Remembering and retrieving
  information; Thinking
  care and feeding of the brain
    aerobic exercise, 65–66
    do puzzles and play games, 65
    eat a well-balanced diet, 66
    get plenty of sleep, 65
    watch the caffeine and alcohol
      consumption, 66
  discussion, 55–57
  learning disabilities, 73–74
  the physical brain, 57–58
Buddhist practices
  "finding the gift," 11
  "mindfulness," 18–19
Budgeting. *See also* Money
  basics
    fixed vs. variable expenses, 202
    focus on your goals, 201

Budgeting *(continued)*
   "Four A's of Budgeting," 202
      income and expenses, 202
      key terms, 201
      savings, 201
   how to budget, 202–204
   sample worksheet, 205–207

**C**
Caffeine use, 66, 108, 185–186
Careers. *See* Job hunting process
Child abuse, low self-esteem and, 6
Cigarette smoking. *See* Smoking
Cleaning the microwave, time-saving tips for, 126
Color, visual learners, 77
Communication. *See also* Listening
   body language, 134
   evaluate your tone of voice, 135
   importance of, 133–134
   multicultural differences, 134–135
   "personal space," 135
   "selective attention," 135–136
   style of, 136
Conflict resolution
   always stay in the present, 144
   dealing with teachers, 146
   listening, 147
   manage the situation, 144–145
   share a good feeling with the other person, 145
   taking things personally, 144
   use self-control, 145
   ways to break the chain of anger, 145–146
Cooking, time-saving tips for, 124–125
Cover letter, 228–230
Credit
   cards
      glossary of terms, 214
      paying off your debt, 214–215
      selecting, 212–213
      understanding them, 211–212
   credit rating, 210–211
   meanings of, 209–211
   start a credit history, 210
   understanding credit, 210
Critical thinking, 67, 157
Cziksentmihalyi, Mihaly, 16

**D**
Debt, 214–215
Deep breathing
   exercise and, 182
   stress and, 109, 162
Demands of school, 1
Dieting, 176–177
Disabilities, feelings about school and, 2

**E**
Eating disorders
   anorexia nervosa, 177–178
   binge eating, 179
   bulimia nervosa, 178–179
Eating habits, 171–172
Efficiency, keeping a log of, 32–33
E-mailing questions to professors, 91
Emotional well-being, 50
   managing emotions, 62
Employment. *See* Job hunting process
Employment portfolio, 230–231
End-of-day analysis, 35–36
Exercise, 180–183

**F**
Fear of failure, 48
Federal Family Education Loan Program Guide, 221
Feelings, 2, 31–32
Financial aid, 217–218
Flashcards, 77

Flexibility, 19
*Flow: The Psychology of Optimal Experience*, 16

**G**
Game plans, 46–47
Gardner, Harold, 59
Glucose tolerance, impaired, 187
Goal setting, 39–53. *See also* Guiding principles of success; Success
  breaking down into "goal units," 49
  dealing with disappointment, 51–52
  don't set the bar too high, 49
  dreams into goals, 40–41
  finding new goals, 49
  fundamentals of success
    figure out what your gift is, 43
    getting good at something, 42
    getting through the bad times, 42
    know what you want and go after it, 42
    success and money, 42
  long-term goals, 48–49
  process of, 48–49
  set your own goals, not someone else's, 49
  short-term goals, 48
  student goals, 52–53
  success do's and don'ts
    game plans, 46–47
    perfectionism, 45–46
    procrastination, 44
    self-esteem, 47–48
  types of goals, 50–51
Goleman, Daniel, 61, 62
Guided imagery, 99
Guiding principles of success, 13–21
  1. become an active listener, 13–14
  2. thinking outside the box, 14–15
  3. figure out what you find most satisfying, 15–17
  4. create time for things you care about, 17–18
  5. learn to enjoy what's in front of you, 18–19
  6. learn to be flexible, 19
  7. prioritize, 20

**H**
Hobbies, cure for stress, 110
Holistic hints
  body image
    be kind to yourself, 175
    feeling good about yourself, 174–175
    genetic influence, 173
    the issue of, 172–173
    set point for weight, 174
    "will power," 174
  dieting, 176–177
  eating disorders
    anorexia nervosa, 177–178
    binge eating, 179
    bulimia nervosa, 178–179
  exercise, 180–183
  good eating habits, 171–172
  idea of "wholeness," 168
  nutrition
    basic building blocks
      fat intake, 170–171
      fiber, 171
      processed foods, 170
      protein intake, 170–171
      reading labels, 171
    drink water, 169–170
  sleep
    "don'ts," 185–186
    "do's," 184–185
    importance of, 183–184
  sleep deprivation
    driver fatigue, 186–187
    impaired glucose tolerance, 187

Holistic hints *(continued)*
    smoking
        clove cigarettes and smokeless
            tobacco, 192–193
        don't start, 191
        low-tar brands, 191
        reasons to stop now, 190–191
        stopping, 191–192
    substance abuse
        being a friend, 189–190
        effects of, 188–189
        signs, 187–188
Home maintenance, time-saving
    tips for, 128–129

# I

Intelligence, 58–62
    emotional intelligence, 61–62
    recognizing your own, 60–61
    seven basic intelligences
        bodysmart (bodily-kinesthetic
            intelligence), 60
        logic smart (logicomathem
            atical intelligence), 59
        music smart (musical
            intelligence), 60
        people smart (interpersonal
            intelligence), 60
        picture smart (visual-spatial
            acuity), 60
        self-smart (intrapersonal
            intelligence), 60
        word smart (linguistic
            intelligence), 59
Internet research, 89–91
Interpersonal intelligence, 60
Interpersonal relationships, 131–147
    communication
        body language, 134
        evaluate your tone of voice, 135
        importance of, 133–134
        multicultural differences, 134–135

"personal space," 135
        "selective attention," 135–136
        style of, 136
    conflict resolution
        always stay in the present, 144
        dealing with teachers, 146
        listening, 147
        manage the situation, 144–145
        share a good feeling with the
            other person, 145
        taking things personally, 144
        use self-control, 145
        ways to break the chain of
            anger, 145–146
    personality and attitude, 131–133
        anger management, 141–143
        assertiveness, 139
        distinction between, 137
        giving negative feedback, 141
        handling criticism, 140–141
        introvert vs. extrovert, 137–138
        learning tact, 139
        new ways of thinking, 138–139
        "reframing" your attitude, 139
    self-assessment, 132
Interviewing
    ask questions, 236
    extra resumé, 235
    first impressions, 234
    follow-up thank-you note, 237
    preparation, 233–235
    punctuality, 237
    questions interviewers cannot
        ask, 237
    role-playing your interview, 235
Intrapersonal intelligence, 60

# J

Job hunting process
    cover letter, 228–230
    employment portfolio, 230–231
    interviewing
        ask questions, 236

extra resumé, 235
first impressions, 234
follow-up thank-you note, 237
preparation, 233–235
punctuality, 235
questions interviewers cannot
    ask, 237
role-playing your interview, 235
wardrobe, 234
inventory of your skills, 223–225
resumés
    content, 227–228
    presentation, 225–226
salary negotiations, 237–239
targeting employers
    networking, 232
    sources, 231–232
    "Thank you" notes, 232
Journal keeping, 27–37
    activity, 29–30
    efficiency, 32–33
    end-of-day analysis, 35–36
    feelings, 31–32
    start/stop/total, 28–29
    what's my role?, 33–34
Junk food, stress and, 108

**L**

Laughing, when stressed out, 110
Laundry, time-saving tips for,
    127–128
Learning disabilities, 73–74
Library, 88–89
Linguistic intelligence, 59
Listening, 149–158. *See also*
    Communication
    are you guilty of not listening to
        others, 150–152
    the basics
        look at the person you're
            listening to, 155
        motivation and discipline, 154
        nonverbal clues, 154–155

"reflective listening," 155
    talk to people, not at them, 155
in the classroom
    apply critical thinking and ask
        questions, 157
    be intellectually engaged,
        156–157
    changing body position, 156
    get enough sleep, 156
    sit up front, 156
hearing loss, 157–158
importance of learning to listen,
    149–150
practice, 157
why people don't hear each other
    daydreamers, 149–152
    distractions, 153
    feeling socially inadequate, 152
    preconceived notions about
        other people, 153
Logic smart (logicomathematical
    intelligence), 59
Log keeping. *See* Journal keeping

**M**

Mental well-being, 50
Mindfulness, 18–19
Mind-mapping, 73
Money, 195–219
    budgeting
        basics
            fixed vs. variable expenses, 202
            focus on your goals, 201
            "Four A's of Budgeting," 202
            income and expenses, 202
            key terms, 201
            savings, 201
        how to budget, 202–204
        sample worksheet, 205–207
    credit
        credit rating, 210–211
        meanings of, 209–210
        start a credit history, 210

Money *(continued)*
   understanding credit, 210
   credit cards
     glossary of terms, 214
     paying off your debt, 214–215
     selecting, 212–213
     understanding them, 211–212
   financial aid, 217–219
   problems and stress, 109
   psychology of
     being well off vs. being a
       good human being, 198
     the consumer culture, 197–198
     different messages about,
       196–197
     family differences, 197
     the financial pyramid, 199–201
     keeping a well-balanced life,
       198–199
   savings, 208–209
   student loans, 218–219
Motivation
   channeling emotions in the
     service of a goal, 62
   intrinsic, 56
   issues affecting, 2
   School + Motivation =
     Achievement, 56
Music smart (musical intelligence),
   60

## N

National Institute for Drug Abuse
   hotline, 189
Networking, 232
"No," learning how to say it, 25,
   103–107
Noise levels, reducing, 108
Note taking, 85–88
   overview, 86–87
   specific strategies, 87–88
Nutrition
   basic building blocks

fat intake, 170–171
fiber, 171
processed foods, 170
protein intake, 170–171
reading labels, 171
drink water, 169–170

## O

Organizational skills, 113–130. *See
   also* Time tracking
   time management
     excuses, 116–117
     find your "inner organizer," 116
     getting a handle on it, 117–118
     if you are always late, 116
   tips for saving time
     around the house, 125–126
     cleaning the microwave, 126
     cooking, 124–125
     home maintenance, 128–129
     laundry, 127–128
     miscellaneous, 129–130
     shopping, 123–124
     travel, 129
   the "to-do" list
     check off as you go along,
       121–122
     daily/weekly/monthly lists, 119
     grouping things, 119–120
     keep to one side of the page, 119
     make it manageable, 122–123
     organizers, 122
     prioritization, 120–122
     save one block of free time a
       day, 120
     scheduling things, 120
     use a pencil, 119

## P

Parents
   hypercritical, 4, 5
   neglectful, 4
   with unreasonable standards, 8

People smart (interpersonal intelligence), 60
Perfectionism, 45–46
Perkins loan, 218
Personality and attitude, 131–133
  anger management, 141–143
  assertiveness, 139
  distinction between, 137
  giving negative feedback, 141
  handling criticism, 140–141
  introvert vs. extrovert, 137–138
  learning tact, 139
  new ways of thinking, 138–139
  "reframing" your attitude, 139
Physical well–being, 50
Picture smart (visual-spatial acuity), 60
Positive thinking, 9–12
  looking for the gift, 11
  negative thinking and self-fulfilling prophecies, 10
  positive self-talk, 11–12
  secret of, 10
Prioritization, 20, 120–122
Procrastination, 44
Progressive relaxation, 99
Public speaking. *See also* Speaking
  don't apologize, 161–164
  gestures, 164–165
  have a strong opening and closing, 162
  interaction with the audience, 162–163
  know your material, 162
  try deep breathing for anxiety, 162

**R**

"Reflective listening," 155
Relationships
  eliminate unhealthy ones, 108
  handling, 62

Relaxation, progressive, 99
Remembering and retrieving information
  leave a message on your answering machine, 64
  mnemonics, 64
  repeat the information five or six times, 64
  write it down, 63–64
Resumés
  content, 227–229
  presentation, 225–227
Retention, 56

**S**

Salary negotiations, 237–239
School + Motivation = Achievement, 56
Search engines, 90
Self-awareness, 62
Self-esteem, 3–4
  positive thinking, 9–12
  students feelings about, 5–6
  success and, 6–9, 47–48
Self-fulfilling prophecies, 10
Selfishness, 105
Self-smart (intrapersonal intelligence), 60
Self-validation, 4–5
  positive thinking, 9–12
  students feelings about, 5–6
Shopping, time-saving tips for, 123–124
Skills inventory, 223–225
Sleep
  as cure for stress, 109
  deprivation
    driver fatigue, 186–187
    impaired glucose tolerance, 187
  "don'ts," 185–186
  "do's," 184–185
  importance of, 183–184

Smoking
  clove cigarettes and smokeless
    tobacco, 192–193
  don't start, 191
  low-tar brands, 191
  reasons to stop now, 190–191
  stopping, 191–192
Social well-being, 50
Speaking
  commonly mispronounced
    words, 161
  public speaking
    don't apologize, 163
    gestures, 163–164
    have a strong opening and
      closing, 162
    interaction with the audience,
      162–163
    know your material, 162
    try deep breathing for anxiety,
      162
  skills
    don't speak in a monotone, 160
    enunciate, 160
    listen to trained voices, 160
    for non-English speakers,
      164–165
    open your mouth wider, 160
    tone of voice, 158–159
    volume, 159–160
Spiritual well-being, 50–51
Stafford loan, 218–219
Start/stop/total activity, 28–29
Storyboarding, 77
Stress, 99–111. *See also* Test anxiety
  defined, 100
  don'ts, 108–109
  do's, 109–111
  impact of, 101
  recognizing signs of, 103
  relief from, assertiveness,
    103–105
  role it plays in our lives, 101–102

Student Aid Report (SAR), 219
Student loans, 218–219
Study skills, 75–91
  auditory learners, 79
  have a sense of your biological
    clock, 82–84
  Internet research, 89–91
  the library, 88–89
  naps can help, 84
  note taking, 85–88
    overview, 86–87
    specific strategies, 87–88
  a quiet place to study,
    76, 80–81
  tactile/kinesthetic learners,
    79–80
  the textbook, 84–85
  visual learners, 76–77
Substance abuse
  being a friend, 189–190
  effects of, 188–189
  signs, 187–188
Success. *See also* Goal setting;
  Guiding principles of success
  know what you want, 8
  modeling a successful person, 8–9
  parents' unreasonable standards, 8
  positive thinking, 9–12
  self-esteem, 6–9
  your definition of, 7–8

**T**
Tactile/kinesthetic learners, 79–80
Teachers
  conflict resolution, 146
  e-mailing questions to, 91
Test anxiety, 93–99. *See also* Stress
  be prepared mentally and
    physically, 95
  best antidote, 94–95
  sit by yourself, 95
  take a practice exam, 95
  take plenty of time to get to the

test, 95
taking control, 95–97
telltale signs of anxiety, 94
test-taking strategies, 97–98
  instant relaxation methods, 99
  when it's almost over, 97–99
Textbooks, approach to, 84–85
"Thank you" notes, 232, 237
Theory of Multiple Intelligences, 59–60
Thinking
  the creativity factor, 71–73
  critical, 67, 157
  logical, 67–69
  mind-mapping, 73
  outside the box, 14–15
  problem-solving, 69–71
Time tracking, 23–37. *See also* Organizational skills
  creating a log or journal, 27–37
    activity, 29–30
    efficiency, 32–33
    end-of-day analysis, 35–36
    feelings, 31–32
    start/stop/total, 28–29
    what's my role?, 33–34
  developing an awareness of time, 26–27

feeling overwhelmed, 25
learning to say "no," 25
patterns of time use, 24
remember the Seven Guiding Principles, 36–37
work overload, 25
worrying too much, 26
Tobacco use. *See* Smoking
Travel, time-saving tips for, 129

**V**

Visual learners, 76–77
Visual-spatial acuity, 60
Voice, tone of, 155, 158–159. *See also* Speaking

**W**

Wardrobe, 234
"Wholeness," idea of, 168
Words, commonly mispronounced, 161
Word smart (linguistic intelligence), 59

**Y**

Yoga, 109